YOU STAND

STANDING STRONG IN LIFE'S BATTLES

CHRISTA MADRID

© 2021 Christa Madrid

Scripture taken from the New King James
Version unless otherwise noted.

Scripture taken from the New King James Version.
Copyright © 1982 by Thomas Nelson, Inc.
Used by permission. All rights reserved.

Scripture quotations taken from the Amplified® Bible
(AMPC), Copyright © 1954, 1958, 1962, 1964, 1965,
1987 by The Lockman Foundation. Used by permission.

Scripture quotations taken from the Amplified®
Bible (AMP), Copyright © 2015 by The Lockman
Foundation. Used by permission.

Holy Bible, New Living Translation, copyright ©
1996, 2004, 2015 by Tyndale House Foundation.
Used by permission of Tyndale House Publishers, Inc.,
Carol Stream, Illinois 60188. All rights reserved.

*To Jesus, the Lord of my victory.
To Michael, for standing with me.
To all those fighting the good fight of faith.*

CONTENTS

Introduction vii
Chapter 1: You Stand in Battle 1
Chapter 2: You Stand in Your Redemption. 23
Chapter 3: You Stand on God's Word. 36
Chapter 4: You Stand by Faith 53
Chapter 5: You Stand with Christ's Authority. 71
Chapter 6: You Stand without Fear. 83
Chapter 7: You Stand with Praise and Thanksgiving. 104
Chapter 8: You Stand in Love and Forgiveness 119
Chapter 9: You Stand in His Strength 132
Chapter 10: You Stand without Giving Up. 138
Chapter 11: You Stand with Confidence 147
Conclusion. 165
Prayer for Salvation 168
Appendix A: My Confession of Faith 170
Appendix B: Characteristics of Those Who Live by Faith . 177
Appendix C: Scriptures to Stand On 180
Appendix D: Reasons Not to Fear 189
Connect with the Author 191

INTRODUCTION

A WOUNDED SOLDIER struggles up a rocky mountain dazed and breathless. His shirt is ripped and bloodied, his belt broken and dangling from his belt-loops. Beneath his soiled camouflage pants, his legs bear the marks of days of battle as he crawls to safety through sharp undergrowth. His boots, muddied and torn, look like they couldn't survive another day. His machine gun, once full of ammo, hangs loosely from his shoulder. He didn't have the strength to use it, even if he had to. Worst of all, his head is bare, for he had lost his helmet to a flying bullet. His face is bruised and bloodied, his downcast countenance revealing what a lengthy battle it has been. All he wants now is to reach the top of the mountain and collapse. He just wishes the battle would end. He doesn't have much more fight left in him.

Can you identify with this soldier? The doctor gives you a negative health diagnosis. Your spouse wants a divorce, and your kids have rejected your authority. You've lost your job and don't have enough money to cover the bills you already have, much less the future ones. Your mind is plagued day and night with stress and worry. How will you ever survive this? You feel like you're in a war ... and losing fast.

If you've been war-torn because of life's battles, you are not alone. Every Christian has been the target of Satan's attacks. His greatest joy is to attack the lives of every believer on the globe, the ones God calls His children. He fulfills John 10:10a with sharp accuracy: "The thief does not come except to steal, and to kill, and to destroy ..." His schemes usually don't end with just a few skirmishes, either. As your ultimate enemy, he wants to destroy you with *many* afflictions.

> Many are the afflictions of the righteous, but the Lord delivers him out of them all (Psalm 34:19).

> "These things I have spoken to you, that in Me you may have peace. In the world you will have tribulation; but be of good cheer, I have overcome the world" (John 16:33).

God, however, desires that you recover. But do more than recover; learn to stand triumphant on the top of your mountain. He wants you to come out stronger so you can fulfill His call for your life and help someone else in their battles. You can win, but it takes knowing, understanding, and utilizing the weapons and ammo He's provided (Ephesians 5:17). You must have the will and heart of a soldier, fighting for what rightfully belongs to you.

Are you ready to run instead of crawl through life's trials? Do you desire to stand strong in victory rather than experience defeat in every battle? Through God's grace it *is* possible! This book is written to show you how to access that grace by putting His Word into action. It will show you how to respond when you're attacked, and how to stand daily at attention so the enemy doesn't get the upper hand. You will learn:

- what true faith looks like and how to exercise it
- how to use the authority and weapons God's given you
- who you are in Christ so you won't believe Satan's lies
- how to walk in God's strength by not relying on your own
- how to rejoice regardless of how dark the challenge seems
- how to persevere fearlessly until you see your victory

As you choose to exercise each step, you will grow in confidence in knowing who you are, and the authority God has given you. You will soar with the knowledge of God's power working for you, in you, and through you. Battles will no longer look as daunting, and life's problems will shrink in the light of God's Word. As a result, you will see God power heal your body and mend your broken relationships. You will experience God's unfailing love as He supplies every need you have. Joy and peace will replace stress, driving out all fear and frustration. You will come out the victor rather than the defeated—God's soldier standing strong!

CHAPTER 1

YOU STAND IN BATTLE

IN CONCLUSION, BE strong in the Lord [be empowered through your union with Him]; draw your strength from Him [that strength which His boundless might provides]. Put on God's whole armor [the armor of a heavy-armed soldier which God supplies], that you may be able successfully to stand up against [all] the strategies *and* the deceits of the devil. For we are not wrestling with flesh and blood [contending only with physical opponents], but against the despotisms, against the powers, against [the master spirits who are] the world rulers of this present darkness, against the spirit forces of wickedness in the heavenly (supernatural) sphere. Therefore put on God's complete armor, that you may be able to resist *and* stand your ground on the evil day [of danger], and, having done all [the crisis demands], to stand [firmly in your place]. Stand therefore [hold your ground], having tightened the belt of truth around your loins and having put on the breastplate of integrity *and* of moral rectitude *and* right standing with God, and having shod your feet in preparation [to face the enemy with the firm-footed stability, the promptness, and the readiness produced by the good news] of the Gospel of peace. Lift up over all the [covering] shield of saving faith, upon which you can quench all the flaming missiles of the wicked [one]. And take the helmet of salvation and the sword that the Spirit wields, which is the Word of God. Pray at all times (on every occasion, in every season) in the Spirit, with all [manner of] prayer and entreaty. To that end keep alert and watch with strong purpose *and* perseverance, interceding in behalf of all the saints (God's consecrated people) (Ephesians 6:10-18, AMPC).

THE REAL ENEMY

As you go through life and experience hardship, it is important to know the root cause of your problems. Without understanding their source, you won't know who or what you're against, when to give in or when to fight. Ephesians 6 is clear that your enemy is the devil. He's not physical but spiritual. You are not fighting against people, germs, or even nature. Your struggle is with him and his armies. Even his name is Abaddon and Apollyon, which means Destroyer (Revelation 9:11).

"The thief does not come except to steal, and to kill, and to destroy. I have come that they may have life, and that they may have it more abundantly" (John 10:10).

God and the devil have been opposite since the beginning of time when the devil rebelled and was cast from heaven (Isaiah 14:12-17, Ezekiel 28:11-19). Starting with the Garden of Eden, Satan has done nothing but wreak evil in the world through his sinful nature. He turned Adam and Eve against God through disobedience (Genesis 3). From that day on, sin, sickness, poverty, and violence have been a part of life in this world (Romans 5:17a). God's perfect and good creation had been marred by one man's decision. His "will be done on earth as it is in heaven" no longer reigns ... if man chooses the devil over God.

Let's be clear: God is not the author of your hardship. If God were the source of your problems, Ephesians 6 would be commanding us to fight and stand against God. He, however, is only good; no evil or darkness can be found in Him (1 John 1:5). Genesis 1 is clear that everything God created was good and pure, and only after the devil arrived on the scene did it turn bad. From that day forward, God urged His people to believe in Him and act in obedience to His Word. At last, He sent His only Son Jesus to permanently strip the devil of his power through His sacrifice. It started with His earthly ministry and finished on the cross.

You may know that sin is from the devil, but often

the blame for sickness or some other tragedy is placed on God. Jesus, however, defeated both sin and sickness on the cross (Isaiah 53:5, 6; 1 Peter 2:24). Galatians 3:13 says you've been redeemed (bought back) from the curses found in Deuteronomy 28, which include hardship and destruction in every area of life. The curse of the law was the judgement for sin, the refusal to serve and obey God. Jesus, however, bore that judgement for you on the cross so you didn't have to. He *became* that curse, ending its authority over your life when you received Jesus as your Lord and Savior.

> Christ has redeemed us from the curse of the law, having become a curse for us (for it is written, "Cursed *is* everyone who hangs on a tree") … (Galatians 3:13).

To make it even clearer in our modern vocabulary:

> But Christ has rescued us from the curse pronounced by the law. When he was hung on the cross, he took upon himself the curse for our wrongdoing. For it is written in the Scriptures, "Cursed is everyone who is hung on a tree" (Galatians 3:13, NLT).

It's obvious that it is not God's will for you to suffer things that were defeated on the cross. Otherwise, Jesus's death, burial, and resurrection would have been partially pointless. Or God is inconsistent in that some days He wants you to experience His redemption, while other days He wants you to experience the devil's curse. On the contrary, oppression of any kind is not from Him. If it's in your life, it is trespassing illegally because Jesus took that curse upon Himself for you. It does not belong to you, and it can only stay if it's allowed to stay.

> ...how God anointed Jesus of Nazareth with the Holy Spirit and with power, who went about doing good and healing all who were oppressed by the devil, for God was with Him (Acts 10:38).
>
> "For the Son of Man did not come to destroy men's lives but to save them" (Luke 9:56a).

Innately, we know what goodness is. Our God-ordained law enforcement knows to stop thieves, murderers, and liars, all sins addressed in the Ten Commandments written by God. We have organizations that protect children from parents who abuse their children. He has told us to pray "your will be done on earth as it is in heaven," knowing that no sickness, death, or sorrow is there. If God expects us to desire and do His will on earth, yet does not do it Himself, He cannot be trusted. He would be a two-faced liar, as evil as Satan. He would be just as double-minded as He commands us not to be (James 1:8). No, God is a good God and a good, perfect Father.

"If you then, being evil [natural], know how to give good gifts to your children, how much more will your Father who is in heaven give good things to those who ask Him!" (Matthew 7:11)

Every good gift and every perfect gift is from above, and comes down from the Father of lights, with whom there is no variation or shadow of turning (James 1:17).

This is the message which we have heard from Him and declare to you, that God is light and in Him is no darkness at all (1 John 1:5).

To declare that the Lord is upright; He is my rock, and there is no unrighteousness in Him (Psalm 9:15).

TRADITIONAL STATEMENTS

Over the years, statements and beliefs have been used to explain the reason why people experience hardship and evil in their lives. They have often put God in a bad light, as if He were the one inflicting the evil. I am going to address some of the most common statements. Through this section, I pray you come to realize that God is only *good* and loves you too much to bring evil into your life.

EVIL IN THE OLD TESTAMENT

"What about the times in the Old Testament when God put diseases and plagues on people?" you might ask. First, those instances were always judgement on sin. People disobeyed Him and the consequence was hardship. Also, many Bible scholars have found that references of judgement from God in the Hebrew are in the permissive sense. He *allowed* it to happen. As a righteous Judge (Psalm 7:11), He could not protect them from something they chose to do that brought them onto the devil's territory. They broke covenant with God and made it clear they wanted to follow their own carnal desires, which was ultimately the devil's desire and nature.

Even then, Lamentations 3:32-33 (NIV) says that He desires compassion over judgement: "Though he brings grief, he will show compassion, so great is his unfailing love. For he does not willingly bring affliction or grief to anyone." In the case of sexual immorality in the church, the Apostle Paul instructed the church to "hand this man over to Satan for the destruction of the flesh, so that his spirit may be saved on the day of the Lord" (1 Corinthians 5:1-5). Clearly, God is not the one who brought the destruction. His greatest desire is that you judge yourself when your born-again spirit convicts you of something you've done wrong: "For if we would judge ourselves, we would not be judged" (1 Corinthians 11:31).

HE GIVETH AND TAKETH AWAY

In Job 1:21, Job says, "… the LORD gave, and the Lord has taken away; blessed be the name of the Lord." People often use this concerning their life's trial, assuming it is God who took away their health, finances, peace, or property. However, Job was mistaken. When you read the book of Job from beginning to end, it's clear that God was not the One who destroyed Job's health, took the lives of his children, and took his property. It was the devil who did the evil, and it was God who restored Job, so he had twice as much as he did before (Job 42:11). Job and his friends were mistaken about a lot of things to the point that God gave them a lecture at the end of the book. But even then, God was merciful to Job and restored him.

It's important to note, too, why Job didn't receive God's protection when the devil attacked him. The clue is in Job 3:25: "For the thing I greatly feared has come upon me, and what I dreaded has happened to me." Fear is not faith in God, but faith in evil. It's impossible to please or receive anything from God with fear canceling out faith in Him (Hebrews 11:6). God had placed a hedge of protection around Job, but that fear gave Satan the legal right to attack Job and his family (Job 1:10-12). Though Satan suggested God destroy Job's family and belongings, this reference and the rest of the book is clear that God gave that license to the devil. God was not the one Who did it.

THE WILDERNESS EXPERIENCE

People sometimes compare their challenging seasons in life to Jesus's "wilderness experience" in Matthew 4:1-11. However, Jesus's experience in the wilderness and the trials you may face are quite different. The wilderness was just a place of isolation to get Jesus away from people. He was fasting and praying, hearing from God concerning His assignment. Unlike the trials sent by the devil to harm us, the Holy Spirit led Jesus into the wilderness for a specific purpose. He had to be tempted to sin by the devil so He could experience what you would experience. He had to go through the temptation "without sin" to be qualified as the perfect sacrifice for our sins. He gave you the perfect example of overcoming it. Because He was tempted and overcame the temptation, He was qualified to aid you in your temptations (Hebrews 2:18, Hebrews 4:15, 16).

Some also believe that Jesus's wilderness experience empowered Him. However, His empowerment came from the Holy Spirit when John the Baptist baptized Him in the Jordan River. Temptation does not make you stronger; but *exercising your faith* in the middle of a temptation, or life's challenges, will. Often when people go through what they call a "wilderness experience," it's not that God led them there or that He is the author of their hardship. It could be that the devil has attacked them, and they need to walk by faith to overcome it. Or it could be a season when they are not sensing God's presence, so they need to trust what His Word says and not what they feel or see.

GOD'S PURPOSE

You may have heard something like, "God has a purpose for it all," indicating that He was the one that created it. As we've discussed, evil comes from the devil. Your hardship is a direct oppression from him. He has a purpose—to destroy you and your effectiveness on this earth. This was his intent when he tempted Adam and Eve. He wanted to destroy God's plan for relationship with man and wanted to establish his own will on the earth. He may use other people and situations to harm you, but the devil is still the author of your trials. God, however, desires that the result of your battle be your victory.

GOD'S LESSON

It is often said that your difficulties are God's way of teaching you a lesson. Though God can use the *opportunity* to teach you valuable things in the middle of crisis, He is not the one who orchestrated it for that purpose. His method of teaching you is through the Holy Spirit and His Word (John 14:26, 2 Timothy 3:16-18). When problems come, the Holy Spirit will remind you of the truth of God's Word. As you read His Word, the Holy Spirit will help you understand the things you need to know to learn and grow. God may even send people to teach you about God's promises applying to your situation. Even then, you must be open to receive that instruction. It's a choice to receive or reject the lesson.

WHAT MAKES YOU STRONGER

You may have also heard, "You will come out stronger after this." This is true, but only under certain conditions. If you will look around you, you will find two different people—those who are stronger after a trial and those who are weaker after a trial. The people who are stronger are the ones who put their trust in God, kept the right attitude, and didn't fall into self-pity. The people who were defeated and came out weaker are the ones who struggled on their own strength and had an attitude of having already lost. As we will study later in this chapter, the choice is up to you. God can use your situation and turn it around for good, but He is not the creator of it.

MORE THAN YOU CAN HANDLE

Another common comment is, "God will never give you more than you can handle." I context, most of the time this is referring to a hardship you may be going through. Like the other comments, it is assuming that your difficulty came from God. We've already proven that God does not give you hardship. Oh, He may assign you to a family, business, vocation, or location that is particularly challenging. People, places, and projects will come with challenges because of human nature and the flaws of the world. But any challenge such as these do not contain the curse of the Law. These challenges can help you grow ... and give you the opportunity to make a difference for the Kingdom of God in the world.

TOGETHER FOR GOOD

Romans 8:28 is an excellent verse to trust in times of struggle: "And we know that all things work together for good to those who love God, to those who are the called according to His purpose." Though God does cause things to work out for your good, there are two details to be aware of concerning this verse. First, for things to work out for your good, you must love God and surrender yourself to His purpose through receiving Jesus as your Lord and Savior. Someone who does not serve God can't expect His intervention because they are not in relationship with Him. Second, in context this verse is referring to the Holy Spirit interceding on your behalf when you are weak and don't know how to pray in trying situations. This, coupled with your covenant promises from God, work together for your good (v. 28-30).

Note that all things outside of the Holy Spirit and your relationship with God *do not* work together for your good. You've seen evil work out for people's demise repeatedly. Good and evil do not work together for good, just like God and the devil do not work together for good. Evil was meant for your demise; God's goodness was meant for your success. God will always cause His Word, His Spirit, and His power to work together for your good, but you have the responsibility to trust Him.

PAUL'S THORN

Paul states in 2 Corinthians 12:7-10 (AMPC) that he was given a "thorn in the flesh." People like to say that his infirmities were the equivalent of disease, perhaps a sight problem left over from his temporary blindness on the road to Damascus. But when you research this passage, you will see this is not necessarily the case.

> "And to keep me from being puffed up *and* too much elated by the exceeding greatness (preeminence) of these revelations, there was given me a thorn (a splinter) in the flesh, a messenger of Satan, to rack *and* buffet *and* harass me, to keep me from being excessively exalted. Three times I called upon the Lord *and* besought [Him] about this *and* begged that it might depart from me; But He said to me, My grace (My favor and lovingkindness and mercy) is enough for you [sufficient against any danger and enables you to bear the trouble manfully]; or *My* strength *and* power are made perfect (fulfilled and completed) *and show themselves most effective* in [your] weakness. Therefore, I will all the more gladly glory in my weaknesses *and* infirmities, that the strength *and* power of Christ (the Messiah) may rest (yes, may pitch a tent over and dwell) upon me! So for the sake of Christ, I am well pleased *and* take pleasure in infirmities, insults, hardships, persecutions,

perplexities *and* distresses; for when I am weak [in human strength], then am I [truly] strong (able, powerful in divine strength).

First, notice that the "thorn in the flesh" was a messenger sent from Satan, not from God. The purpose was to keep Paul from fulfilling his life's calling—the spreading of the Gospel, or revelation, he received from God. In the Young's Literal Translation, Satan is called the Adversary. An adversary is an opponent. Satan was trying to oppose God's work as he has always done. God, of course, would never work against Himself.

In 2 Corinthians 11:23-30, the chapter before his thorn statement, it lists all the trials he went through. Instead of sickness, it lists persecutions, beatings, jail time, shipwrecks, and the pressure of caring for the churches. Even in verse 10, infirmities (also translated weakness or frailty of mind or body) are listed as insults, hardships, persecution, perplexities, and distresses.

The Bible is clear that you are not redeemed from persecution for your faith. In fact, it says it will come (Matthew 10:16-25). Jesus said you would experience it because of your stand for Him. In the time of Paul, hardship for serving Jesus was a normal part of life, much more than it is today in the Western culture. Paul knew this persecution would happen yet continued in the grace provided for Him by God. Expect God's grace in every difficulty in life, but it is for you to stand against the attacks of the devil, not to be overcome by them. The only suffering that you're required to endure in the Kingdom of God is that of persecution from those who oppose the gospel. You have been redeemed of every other hardship as found in Deuteronomy 28 (Galatians 3:13).

YOUR CHARACTER WILL GROW

Romans 5:1-5 and James 1:2-4 talk about how your trials produce perseverance and patience. This is true because that's what God says. But remember, this does not automatically happen to every person who goes through a struggle. Some come out stronger, while others come out weaker. In hardship, you have the *potential* to grow. You excel by choosing to persevere through your battle in faith without giving up. That perseverance produces the character trait of patience, and that patience produces hope—or a confident expectation for your future. The choice is yours: you can be patient in your perseverance, or you can succumb to impatience and miss the hope in your future.

No matter what trying situation comes your way, be solid on who the real source is. Don't allow human tradition to make the Word ineffective in your life (Mark 7:13). Confusion begins with uncertainty; but when you know who your enemy is, you know how to confidently act. Why bother fighting something if it came from God or was God's will for you to be in it? It would be a waste of your time, and ultimately, reap no positive results. The devil would love for you to put the blame on God or someone else. That gives him a greater access into your life so he can continue to steal, kill, and destroy (John 10:10).

THE REAL WEAPONS

Human nature would love to have everything come easy. Push a button and the TV comes on. Talk into your phone and Google tells you an address. Pop your leftovers into a microwave and you've got a meal in minutes. It's all done quickly with little effort.

The Kingdom of God doesn't operate that way, however. Oh, you don't have to work and wait to gain your salvation. That was all accomplished by Jesus on the cross (more about that in the next chapter). But there is a form of work that must be done as a Christian. For instance, the Bible says that faith without works is dead (James 2:20). Love has action, and your salvation must be "worked out" by living a holy life (1 Corinthians 13, Philippians 2:12). As a child of God, you've got your part to play. And in all of these, God will not *make* you do anything. It's your choice.

Many say that "God is in control" and "God is sovereign." These are both true, but only in context. God is sovereign in the sense that He is the supreme ruler possessing supreme power, as the word means. However, just because He reigns doesn't mean His perfect will is done all the time; otherwise, Adam and Eve, the children of Israel, and other rebellious people in the Bible would have been forced to obey Him rather than choosing the devil's lies. He is not a dictator who forces people to do His bidding. God *is* in control—but only if you'll let Him.

When you read through Scripture and note all the times God gave people an instruction, they may or may not have obeyed. God didn't control their actions. They heard His instructions and decided for themselves whether they were going to do it or not. God and other leaders gave instructions such as "choose you this day whom you will serve" (Joshua 24:14-15). God even challenged Israel with statements like "if you will listen diligently to the voice of the Lord your God" and "if you faithfully obey the voice of the Lord your God" (Exodus 15:26, Deuteronomy 28:1). Blessings followed if they chose to do what He said. He did not make them do it, any more than He made you receive Jesus as your Lord and Savior. *You* had to first confess with your mouth and believe with your heart before you received His salvation (Romans 10:9, 10).

The same is true when it comes to receiving the victory and blessings Jesus purchased for you on the cross. You must *do* something in response to what He has already done. Let's look again at Ephesians 6. The given subject of this passage is *you*. *You* be strong. *You* put on the whole armor of God. *You* stand. *You* take up the whole armor of God. *You* pray. Clearly, God is not going to do it for you. You must decide if you will stand and fight, and if you do, what weapons you will use.

> For the weapons of our warfare are not carnal but mighty in God for pulling down strongholds …
> (2 Corinthians 10:4)

Standing alone is useless unless you are dressed in armor with weapons to fight with. The enemy will defeat you if you're not wielding your own weapon and moving forward as you stand. Like Ephesians 6 states, you are not fighting a carnal, or physical, war but a spiritual one. Your weapons have nothing to do with how strong physically you are, how mentally intelligent you are, or how much money you have in the bank. To win this spiritual battle, you must address the spiritual realm by fighting with spiritual weapons with ammunition capable of taking out spiritual forces.

As Ephesians 6 says, it's the whole, or complete, armor that counts. You can't afford to neglect a piece. You must believe and apply it constantly because the devil is constantly looking for ways to attack you. If he finds one opening in your armor, he will aim there, hoping to take you out. Your greatest defense is a strong understanding of who you are as God's child, your trust in Him, and a proper use and belief in His Word.

RIGHTEOUSNESS, SALVATION, AND THE GOSPEL

To win your battles, you need to have a clear understanding of the gospel (good news) and your righteousness (right-standing with God)—all stemming from the salvation message. If you have received Jesus as Lord and Savior, you can have confidence to come before God as His children, your past forgiven and your spirit sin-free before Him. You are His child and heir with nothing to intimidate you (Hebrews 4:14-16; 2 Corinthians 5:21;

Romans 8:16-17). When the devil lies to you, saying you're not good enough to receive God's protection and deliverance, you can boldly refute it because you know where you stand in God's Kingdom.

FAITH

Faith is simply believing and trusting God. It is your greatest defense against the devil. That trust is what enables God to move on your behalf, for He doesn't operate any other way (Hebrews 11; James 1:6-7). When you always trust God in all things, the devil's attacks are stopped. You know too much of God's nature and His Word to stop believing. This—your faith—is the victory that overcomes the world (1 John 5:4)!

THE WORD

God and His Word are inseparable. If you trust God, you will trust His Word. To be a true disciple, God's Word should be the most important part of your life, taking priority over any other word or opinion. By hiding it in your heart, acting on it, and believing it, you have a reservoir of ammo to fight with. The moment the devil tries to attack you with a lie, physical symptom, or negative situation, you can stop him in his tracks by speaking the Word. The devil doesn't stand a chance when that Word is in your mouth like it was in Jesus's (Matthew 4:1-11). Satan has no choice but to flee.

PRAYER

The conclusion to God's armor is prayer, a powerful weapon against the devil. God hears and answers your prayers when you pray in faith according to His will. Whether it be for your own needs or in intercession for others, Ephesians 6:18 is clear that it is powerful in battle. Especially when led by the Holy Spirit, your prayers do "avail much" (James 5:16).

THE REAL BATTLE

Yes, your battle is with the devil, a spiritual force. Yes, you must act by standing, putting on your armor, and using your weaponry. But what exactly is the fight? 1 Timothy 6:12 says, "Fight the good fight of faith, lay hold on eternal life, to which you were also called and have confessed the good confession in the presence of many witnesses."

> Since the devil has already been defeated on the cross (more on this in the next chapter), your fight is not to defeat him. Your battle is to keep your faith unmoved until you see your promise appear in the natural. You must *stay* standing once you've determined to stand. Rest assured, the devil will try to pull you down from your standing position by utilizing his wiles: "Put on the whole armor of God, that you may be able to stand against the wiles, or trickery, of the devil" (Ephesians 6:11).

The devil will do his best to trick you into letting go of your trust, or faith, in God. He will whisper lies of despair and defeat into your ears. He will distract you with the cares of life to break your focus. He will send people to speak words of doubt and unbelief so you will question what you believe. He will torment you with symptoms that seem to deny God's truth. He will do whatever it takes to keep you from standing alert with your armor and your weapons.

That's why 1 Peter 5:8-9 commands: "Be sober, be vigilant; because your adversary the devil walks about like a roaring lion, seeking whom he may devour. Resist him, steadfast in the faith, knowing that the same sufferings are experienced by your brotherhood in the world."

Ephesians 5:15 also says to "see then that you walk circumspectly, not as fools but as wise." Circumspectly means cautiously and attentively. Spiritually, stay aware of everything going on around you. Stay focused on your position of faith, your purpose as a Christian, and your trust in God's Word. You can't afford to get distracted by the devil's lies, other opinions, or the concerns of life. If you do, you will lower your sword, forget to carry your shield, and neglect to put on the rest of your armor. You're an open target then, susceptible to the devil's lies and temptations.

The devil can only devour those who will let him, so you've got to utilize your armor and stay filled with the knowledge of God's Word. Then when he does lie against God's truth, you can detect it in a moment. But you can't stop with simply recognizing his tactics. You can't simply ignore him. You must resist him with the truth of God's Word. You must make it clear where you stand and command him to get off your territory. You may have to do it repeatedly, like Jesus in the wilderness, but you must not tolerate his trickery for a moment.

Is it an easy fight? No. Will you always feel like fighting? Rarely. But according to God's Word, your victory depends on it. You must stand, refusing to move or be detoured. Sure, you might be tempted to get discouraged, distracted, and lose heart from time to time. But if you do, you can always stand to your feet once more, adamant that you will see your victory, regardless of what the battleground looks like. God is on your side (Psalm 108:13)!

CHAPTER 2

YOU STAND IN YOUR REDEMPTION

AS WE'VE CONCLUDED, the devil is your enemy. You must fight him with spiritual weapons so you can have the victory promised to you. But someone had to make a way to make those weapons available to you. On your own, you would be powerless against the devil because the only weapons you had were natural. You could yell insults, throw grenades, and shoot guns and be totally ineffective. Without official authority backing up even effective spiritual weapons, the devil would only laugh because there was no power behind your battle plan. He'll only submit to weapons that contain the power to defeat.

Gratefully, God knew of your need and planned your victory before the world began—a plan executed on the cross (Revelation 13:8). The ultimate battle has already been won through Jesus's death, burial, resurrection. The devil has been permanently defeated! He must submit to what has been accomplished on the cross ... and everything done in its authority.

> And you, being dead in your trespasses and the uncircumcision of your flesh, He has made alive together with Him, having forgiven you all trespasses, having wiped out the handwriting of requirements that was against us, which was contrary to us. And He has taken it out of the way, having nailed it to the cross. *Having disarmed principalities and powers, He made a public spectacle of them, triumphing over them in it* (Colossians 2:13-15, italics added).

> Inasmuch then as the children have partaken of flesh and blood, He Himself likewise shared in the same, that through death He might *destroy him who had the power of death, that is, the devil, and release those who through fear of death were all their lifetime subject to bondage* (Hebrews 2:14-15, italics added).

> "The Spirit of the Lord is upon Me, because He has anointed Me to preach the gospel to the poor; He has sent Me to heal the brokenhearted, to *proclaim liberty to the captives and recovery of sight to the blind, to set at liberty those who are oppressed; to proclaim the acceptable year of the Lord*" (Luke 4:18-19, italics added).

The exciting fact is that Jesus did it "once for all" (Hebrews 10:10)! Jesus declared from the cross "it is finished" (John 19:20), a statement that declared that you don't have to be like the Israelites who consistently had to make sacrifices to keep themselves right with God. They didn't have to tiptoe through rituals to be in a good standing with God. Because Jesus sacrificed Himself, the price for your right-standing with God has been paid. The devil's rule in your life has been defeated, without the need to do it again.

YOUR INHERITANCE

According to Romans 8:17, you are child, an heir of God, when you received Jesus as Lord and Savior. An heir is one who is legally entitled to another's possessions after their death. You became a legal heir to all that God has when you became part of His family. He adopted you, making you His child (Ephesians 1:5). "The Spirit Himself bears witness with our spirit that we are children of God, and if children, then heirs—heirs of God and joint heirs with Christ, if indeed we suffer with Him, that we may also be glorified together" (Romans 8:17).

As God's heir, the victory Jesus gained for you on the cross also includes an inheritance. This inheritance is reserved in heaven for you and will not decay or fade away with time (1 Peter 1:3-5). It contains multiple benefits, or blessings, that God originally intended for you before Adam and Eve's fall. It also includes the victory over the devil should he try to steal those blessings away. To win your battle, you need to understand all these benefits found in your redemption—what they made you to be, put you in, gave you, and enabled you to do.

As discussed in the first chapter, evil came into the world when the devil was given reign over it. Sickness, poverty, violence, and death became the norm. Jesus came to reverse that curse by becoming a curse in your place so you could have His blessings upon receiving Him as Lord and Savior (Galatians 3:13-14). If you will look at Deuteronomy 28, which includes the curse of the law, you will find curses that include everything you would deem evil—sickness, poverty, violence, and death. Jesus, however, as your substitute, took all of it on Himself. When you received that substitute by asking Jesus to be your Lord and Savior, you were given freely "all things that pertain to life and godliness":

> Grace and peace be multiplied to you in the knowledge of God and of Jesus our Lord, as His divine power has given to us all things that pertain to life and godliness, through the knowledge of Him who called us by glory and virtue, by which have been given to us exceedingly great and precious promises, that through these you may be partakers of the divine nature, having escaped the corruption that is in the world through lust (2 Peter 1:3-4).

To be a "partaker of the divine nature" means you

were born again when you received Jesus as your Lord and Savior (John 3:7). Your old nature was replaced by God's nature on the inside of you.

> For "whoever calls on the name of the Lord shall be saved" (Romans 10:13).
>
> For by grace you have been saved through faith, and that not of yourselves; it is the gift of God, not of works, lest anyone should boast (Ephesians 2:8, 9).

The Greek word "saved" in these verses means to save, deliver, protect, heal, preserve, and to make whole. All of this was done for you on the cross. The first step to receive the benefits of salvation is to receive Jesus as your Lord and Savior. Then to receive the benefits of salvation, you must believe in what it includes and fight anything that would try to steal it from you. It's your inheritance "reserved in heaven for you" (1 Peter 1:4). The devil is the master thief, but he can only take what he can steal. When the devil tries to throw a "fiery dart" of anything less than what's included in your salvation, reject it and count is as outside of God's will for your life (Ephesians 6:16). Jesus spent too much by coming to earth and dying on the cross for you to receive less than His sacrifice purchased for you—your inheritance of provision, healing, and protection.

At the end of this book, you will find in the Resources section a list called "My Confession of Faith." This lists what God is to you, what you have, who you are, and what you can do now that you are a child and an heir of God. I recommend that you review these consistently to keep yourself strong in your walk with God. I'm going to review them, but for the sake of space, I will look at the ones most pertinent to life's battles.

WHAT HE MADE YOU

What has your new status in Christ made you to be? As a Christian, you are so much more than you realize! As we've discussed, God didn't just make you His child; He made you His royal heir. That royalty is a position of power that enables you to reign in life, rather than be defeated in it. God wants you to believe these truths and see yourself just as He has made you to be. It did, after all, cost Him the life of His Son to give you these titles. When you do stand and act out of your royal position as a child of the King of kings, confidence will rise to fight every battle to the very end. The devil may say you are the opposite of these, but you know the truth and stand on it.

- You are a new creation (2 Corinthians 5:17).
- You are redeemed (Galatians 3:13-14).
- You are delivered (Colossians 1:12-14).
- You are blessed (Ephesians 1:3).
- You are healed by Jesus's stripes (1 Peter 2:24).
- You are an overcomer (1 John 5:4-5).
- You are a citizen of heaven (Philippians 3:20).

- You are a member of Christ's body, the church (Ephesians 5:30).
- You are an ambassador for Christ (2 Corinthians 5:20).
- You are complete in Him who is the head of all principality and power (Colossians 2:10).
- You are a king and priest unto God (Revelation 1:6).

WHAT HE GAVE YOU

Like we learned before, He gave His Son *and* His blessings. Those blessings are greater in value than you may realize. Without them, you would be defeated every day because His gifts were meant to bring your success. They include both spiritual and natural blessings because God knew you needed them both.

- You have the anointing of the Holy Spirit abiding in you (1 John 2:27).
- You have the power of the Holy Spirit upon you (Acts 1:8).
- You have the manifestation of the Holy Spirit (1 Corinthians 12:7).
- You have authority over the devil and his works (Luke 10:19).
- You have the right to use the name of Jesus (John 16:23-24; John 14:12-13).

- You have everything you ask in prayer according to God's will (1 John 5:14-15).
- You have deliverance from enemies and freedom from fear (Luke 1:74-75).
- You have the victory (1 Corinthians 15:57).
- You have the Spirit of power, love, and a sound mind (2 Timothy 1:7).
- You have the faith of God (Romans 12:3).
- You have access into God's grace (Romans 5:2).
- You have exceeding great and precious promises (2 Peter 1:4).
- You have an abundant life (John 10:10).
- You have all your needs met according to God's riches in glory by Christ Jesus (Philippians 4:19).
- You have the treasure of God's life and nature in your mortal body (2 Corinthians 4:7).

WHAT YOU CAN DO

You may *feel* like you don't have what it takes to overcome your life's trials, that you're weak and powerless. It may *look* like you're already a loser. But God has made you capable of so much more than simply surviving in battle. He has made you capable of reigning ... if you will trust Him and draw from His power working for you and in you. And this is not just for your benefit; it is for the benefit of others as well.

- You can do all things through Christ who strengthens you (Philippians 4:13).
- You can do the works of Christ (Mark 16:15-18, John 14:12-14).
- You can reign in life (Romans 5:17).

THE GOD INSIDE

In the Christian world, you may have heard songs or sermons expressing how we want God to come down and be with us, showing Himself strong in our situation. Unfortunately, we are asking for the wrong thing. God has already come down. We don't need to wait for Him to show up; He is already here with us (Hebrews 13:5, Matthew 28:20). Through the cross, God has already accomplished and provided everything needed to make Himself available to us. In fact, He is much more than just *with* us—He is *for* us and *in* us.

Knowing and believing this will enable to you to do battle confidently and fearlessly because you know Who's on your side. His attributes are the same today as they were when the Bible was written. God has not and will not change (Malachi 3:6). Jehovah is His name—and He is more than enough for us and your situations. As His child, you have every right to draw from His powerful and perfect nature.

- He is the Lord your righteousness (Jeremiah 23:5-6).

- He is the Lord Who sanctifies you (Leviticus 20:8).
- He is the Lord your peace (Judges 6:23-24).
- He is the Lord Who will provide for you (Genesis 22:14).
- He is the Lord Who heals you (Exodus 15:26).
- He is the Lord your banner, our victory (Exodus 17:15).
- He is the Lord your shepherd (Psalm 23:1).
- He is the Lord Who is present with you (Ezekiel 48:35).

HE IS WITH YOU

Often in hardship it may seem like you're alone. No improvement seems apparent to your physical eyes, and you may not sense any comfort or love. It appears that He has left you. This is not the case. What you feel or see is not an indication of where God is and what He is doing. He has promised His consistent presence in His Word, even though you may not perceive it in the natural. Ignore the feelings—or lack of them—and go by what He alone says. His Name is Immanuel, "God with Us" (Matthew 1:23). You are never alone!

- He is with you and will never leave you (Hebrews 13:5, Matthew 28:20, Isaiah 41:10).
- He is present when people are gathered in His Name (Matthew 18:20).

- His Spirit—the Comforter—will stay with you forever (John 14:16).

HE IS FOR YOU

That God sent His only Son to earth to die for you is proof enough that He is for you. Even in the Old Testament, He was for His children. He loved them and mercifully worked on their behalf, even when they sinned. As His child, He is no less on your side!

- God is for you, so no one can be against you (Romans 8:31).
- Your enemies retreat because God is for you (Psalm 56:9).

HE IS IN YOU

God, in all His perfection and power, is also *in* you. There used to be a time when God was only *with* His people. In the Old Testament, God would reveal Himself to them through miracles, nature, prophets, and sometimes physical appearances of Himself. If the children of Israel were following Him, God never left them. However, His people did not experience God *in* them until the miracle of the New Birth and the infilling of the Holy Spirit on the Day of Pentecost (Acts 2). Now His abiding nature is both *with* you and *in* you.

- His power dwells and works in you
  (Ephesians 3:20, Romans 8:11).
- His Son, the hope of glory, lives in you
  (Colossians 1:27).
- The Holy Spirit lives in you
  (1 Corinthians 3:16).

Because of the Blood of Jesus, you have every title, position, and ability you need to overcome. You take God and His power wherever you go. When you believe this, boldness comes and your view of your situation changes—it becomes smaller and less significant against the greatness of God. You won't overcome, however, if you believe you're nothing, have nothing, and can do nothing—that God is nowhere nearby. These lies alone will defeat you. You're defeated before you even begin the battle.

The devil wants you to believe that you are defeated and barely making it—that you are merely a survivor of past battles. He wants you to believe that you'll never win, or never win again. He will tell you things that are opposite of the truth—what God says. He will remind of you of past sins even though you've repented, and God says you're forgiven. He will bring your attention to your ailing body, even though God's Word says you're healed. He will tell you that you're insignificant and useless in the Kingdom of God, despite the value God's placed on your life. He will plant fearful thoughts in your mind concerning severe weather and violence, regardless of Psalm 91's promise to protect you. He'll try to convince you that your acts of love toward others is pointless as you work toward mending relationships.

When he does this, don't sit idly by and let him chatter. Stand boldly and declare what God says and tell him to leave. You can't afford to listen to lies when the truth of God's Word declares you are royalty and have every victory based on your redemption. You are so much *more* than a survivor; you are more than a conqueror because of His love for you (Romans 8:37)! This is true, not because of how you feel, but because it's what *God* says about you! Knowing and acting on these truths will set you high above the storms on a foundation not easily moved!

CHAPTER 3

YOU STAND ON GOD'S WORD

EVERY STRONG BUILDING needs a foundation, no matter what city, state, or country you live in. Downtown New York skyscrapers and apartment complexes require foundations. English country barns and grain silos stand on foundations. Our homes stand on a foundation, even if it's the size of a backyard. Why? Because without a foundation, the building would begin to sink, shift, and eventually fall. Foundations ensure that the edifice stands, regardless of the weather.

Just like a house needs a foundation, so your life needs a foundation—something that keeps you unmoving when life's challenges hit. According to God's Word, you have two choices: a foundation of rock or a foundation of sand.

"So everyone who hears these words of Mine and acts upon them [obeying them] will be like a sensible (prudent, practical, wise) man who built his house upon the rock. And the rain fell and the floods came and the winds blew and beat against that house; yet it did not fall, because it had been founded on the rock. And everyone who hears these words of Mine and does not do them will be like a stupid (foolish) man who built his house upon the sand. And the rain fell and the floods came and the winds blew and beat against that house, and it fell—and great *and* complete was the fall of it. (Matthew 7:24-27, AMPC).

Storms will come in life, like it or not (Psalm 34:19). What foundation you choose determines whether you will stand or fall, whether you are wise or foolish. A wise person builds their house on the foundation of God's Word by gratefully hearing and acting on what it says. A foolish person ignores God's Word and puts their confidence on their own faulty intellect or the world's solutions. One choice is solid because it comes from a faultless God; the other is shaky because it's based on human imperfections. One can stand tall in a storm while the other can do nothing but fall under pressure.

The difference between these two men's experiences is not the storm they went through. They went through the same storm. The difference is in what they valued. The foolish man is like many who considers the Bible as simply a book, pages with letters and numbers. It sits on his coffee table or beside his bed, only occasionally opened. And when he does open it, it's to glance through a few verses while his mind wonders to what he thinks is his life's more pressing priorities. It might get a little of his attention once or twice a week at church, but his heart is more loyal and attentive elsewhere. He might hear it but does not value it enough to obey it and apply it to his life.

The wise man, however, is like Job and David who knew nothing was as valuable as God's Word. He values it so much that he treasures it more than food and desires it more than fine gold (Job 23:12, Psalm 19:10-11). These two examples express necessity and a pursuit of something valuable. A wise man will not only value it but will look to it as his primary source of wisdom and solution. He has confidence in its ability to impact his life for good and will do what it says.

Ignorance of what God's Word says and not acting on it can hinder you from experiencing God's blessings and receiving the help you need. It's impossible to trust God if you don't first have a promise from Him concerning His will for you. Trusting God is having faith in Him and what He has said (we'll talk more on this in the next chapter). But if you don't know what He has promised, you will have nothing to trust, nothing specific to stand on. That's why seeking out His will in your situation is so crucial if you're are going to receive anything from Him.

God's first and most important communication of His will is found in His Word. Even though some things aren't so specific, God's Word upholds principles that never change and will always stand (Matthew 24:35). For instance, you won't find what specific medical treatment to go through, what method of getting out of debt to choose, or what natural means to utilize when storm-proofing your home. But you will find the foundational principles to help lead the way.

All forms of direction—communication from the Holy Spirit, prophecy, or what you sense your spirit telling you to do—must always line up with what His Book is saying. If it does not, these forms are simply from someone's natural mind. But if it can be backed by God's Word, you can trust its accuracy. In the case of getting through problems that are clearly from the devil, you need to find Scripture that declares it's God's will for you to have the victory. If you need healing, for instance, you need to find Scriptures that promise healing as God's will for you. If you need your bank full or relationships repaired, search the Bible for the Scriptures that back up your need (I've included Scriptures on key subjects in the Resources section at the back of this book). Study them until you're convinced of their power and believe them with all your heart (Hebrews 4:12). Expect them to do what God said it will do!

While in a Sunday night church service, God spoke to me in a strong tone: "My words will not return void!" Though I didn't see anything with my physical eyes or hear anything audibly, I sensed that He was standing in front of me. He wasn't angry but urgent. I knew He wanted me to study out the origin of that verse and all it meant. The phrase He quoted came from Isaiah 55:11, AMPC:

> "So shall My word be that goes forth out of My mouth: it shall not return to Me void [without producing any effect, useless], but it shall accomplish that which I please *and* purpose, and it shall prosper in the thing for which I sent it."

The backstory to this chapter is that Israel was in captivity. God began to foretell through His prophets that their deliverance would come through a Messiah. He called for their repentance and ended the chapter with an encouraging promise of salvation and prosperity. He promised that every Word He had spoken would flourish wherever it fell—it wouldn't be useless or without result. It was powerful and would accomplish incredible things.

As I studied verses 8-13, I came away with these truths:

GOD'S WAYS ARE GREATER THAN OURS

Like Israel, God has called you to seek Him, to turn away from what you think is best. He also stresses that His way includes the power of His Words. His ways are supernatural, including sending *the* Word, His Son Jesus (John 1:1).

"For My thoughts are not your thoughts, neither are your ways My ways, says the Lord. For as the heavens are higher than the earth, so are My ways higher than your ways and My thoughts than your thoughts" (Isaiah 55:8-9, NKJV).

HIS WORD IS POWERFUL AND PURPOSEFUL

Like rain is sent to soak the earth, so the purpose of God's Word is to benefit you! It causes health, growth, and multiplication in your life. It causes your needs to be met and everything around you to prosper—to push forward, break out, and be profitable. His Word does not partially complete anything; it accomplishes *everything* He intended. It will do what *He* pleases, not what another person desires.

"For as the rain and snow come down from the heavens, and return not there again, but water the earth and make it bring forth and sprout, that it may give seed to the sower and bread to the eater, so shall My word be that goes forth out of My mouth: it shall not return to Me void [without producing any effect, useless], but it shall accomplish that which I please *and* purpose, and it shall prosper in the thing for which I sent it" (Isaiah 55:10-11, AMPC).

HIS WORD WILL INSPIRE JOY

Like a plant blooming under the nourishing rain, so God's Word inspires a reason for you to celebrate. Another person's word may make you feel good for a moment, but God's Word will fill you with joy—something that does not fade away because it's not based on emotions and feelings.

> "For you shall go out [from the spiritual exile caused by sin and evil into the homeland] with joy and be led forth [by your Leader, the Lord Himself, and His word] with peace; the mountains and the hills shall break forth before you into singing, and all the trees of the field shall clap their hands" (Isaiah 55:12, AMPC).

HIS WORD WILL TURN BAD INTO GOOD

Whatever you may be facing, God's Word has the power to turn it around for something good. It will be beautiful, with no sign of the old. It will be an unchanging testimony to everyone around you.

> "Instead of the thorn shall come up the cypress tree, and instead of the brier shall come up the myrtle tree; and it shall be to the Lord for a name of renown, for an everlasting sign [of jubilant exaltation] and memorial [to His praise], which shall not be cut off" (Isaiah 55:13, AMPC).

Isaiah 55 isn't the only passage that lists the attributes

and benefits of God's Word. Here are just a few more that you need and should desire:

- Brings life and health (Proverbs 3:8)
- Cleanses your way (Psalm 119:9)
- Brings revival and strength (Psalm 119:25, 28)
- Equips you for the ministry (2 Timothy 3:16-17)
- Gives you guidance (Psalm 119:105)
- Gives you hope (Romans 15:4)
- Brings you blessing (Psalm 112:1)

Considering these, you should feel inspired to make God's Word the foundation of your life! Not only does it live and abide forever (1 Peter 1:23), but it also comes with genuine goodness that you can't find anywhere else. This Word provides and accomplishes things that counterfeits may try to duplicate elsewhere; but they will eventually wither away because they are not genuine. While another person's word may seem to hold so much promise, God's Word is overflowing with power that will produce!

WHAT TO DO WITH THE WORD

In a previous section, we briefly saw how Job and David greatly treasured God's word. If you valued the Word of God in the same way, your attitude would look completely opposite from the foolish man's. It wouldn't be simply a book to you, sitting idly on a bed stand while your mind wanders to other priorities. Joshua 1:8 and Proverbs 4:20-22 are two of the greatest examples of what valuing the Word looks like:

> This Book of the Law shall not depart from your mouth, but you shall meditate in it day and night, that you may observe to do according to all that is written in it. For then you will make your way prosperous, and then you will have good success (Joshua 1:8).

> My son, attend to my words; consent *and* submit to my sayings. Let them not depart from your sight; keep them in the center of your heart. For they are life to those who find them, healing *and* health to all their flesh (Proverbs 4:20-22, AMPC).

According to these verses, God expects you to do more than just read it; He expects you to study it, speak it, meditate on it, and act on it. Only then will you experience *true* success—in any area of life, including winning life's battles. It's serious—serious enough that God made significant effort to get it down on paper over thousands of years. And He was powerful enough to preserve it so you can "make your way prosperous" and "have good success." It simply takes your personal effort and time—but it is well worth it.

God's desire is that you give the same attention to His Word in times of peace as you do in times of crisis. He wants a close relationship with you, and when you pursue His Word, you are pursuing Him. He also knows that if you're not strong in His Word before the storms come, it will be more difficult to build yourself up in the middle of the battle. When you hit those stormy times, it's time to double up on Proverbs 4:20-22 and Joshua 1:8. Especially in times of trouble, you need to know what God says about your situation so you can continue to stand with confidence on your foundation. How do you know what God says? By studying His Word.

READ IT

Again, you won't know God's will until you put your eyes on the Bible's pages, paying close attention to what it says. And when you do read it, you want to read it thoroughly, regardless of whether you're reading two verses or ten chapters. You may not always feel like it, but the outcome of your reading will be worth every minute. The key is to begin with an open heart and a desire to learn.

LISTEN TO IT

Secular education experts unknowingly agree with the Word of God when they say that one of the most important ways to learn something is using all your senses. God's Word doesn't just say to read it. It also says that "faith comes by hearing" (Romans 10:17). If you want to get your mind and spirit engaged in God's Word, read it out loud to yourself. Listen to ministers as they share the Word, in church or on media. You can also listen to

Scripture recordings while doing household chores, driving in the car, etc. You won't regret it!

THINK DEEPLY ON IT

In biblical terms, thinking deeply on God's Word is a simplified way of saying "meditate" (Joshua 1:8). Meditate means to speak and revolve in the mind. It's more than giving it a casual thought. It's contemplation and reflection on a subject followed by speaking to yourself about it. In the case of God's Word, you want to study it, speak it out loud, and consider everything about it so it gets engrained in your thoughts and heart.

HIDE IT IN YOUR HEART

Psalm 119:11 says, "Your word I have hidden in my heart, that I might not sin against You." Having something hidden in your heart is vital to your spiritual walk. When something is hidden away, it makes it difficult, if not impossible, for someone to steal it away. You thoroughly believe it and make it part of who you are. The devil would love to steal it away because he knows that Word is life to you. But like in the parable of the sower that you'll study later, if the Word is deeply rooted in the soil of your heart, the devil cannot steal it away. You will go from victory to victory because it's the foundation of what you believe!

SPEAK IT

Your words are powerful, especially when they are God's words that are spoken. They move mountains, bring life or death, and steer your life in whatever direction you choose (Mark 11:23, Proverbs 18:21, James 3:1-10). From a learning standpoint, speaking God's Word helps you retain what you are reading and studying (more about your words in the next chapter).

ACT ON IT

The next step is to be a doer and not just a hearer of the Word—to act like you believe it's true (James 1:22). Your actions come from a heart of confidence, willing to prepare based on what you *know* is going to happen. Whatever you do, let your actions be out of a heart of faith and not of desperation. Desperation clouds your judgment, hinders your ability to hear from God, and causes you to make wrong decisions. Faith isn't desperate—unless it's desperate to do God's will. It rests, knowing God will do all things well in His timing and in His way (more on this in another chapter).

THE SOIL YOU CHOOSE

As stated before, when you put these things into action during the calm times, you will already be strong when the challenging times come. In other words, if you're not studying God's Word regularly, when the devil attacks, you won't have any ammo on hand to fight with. But if you're constantly studying and growing in God's Word, your ammo clip will remain full. This makes it harder for the devil to overcome you with hardship and makes the battle less difficult. When you enter already strong, all that is required is to maintain your ground. However, if you haven't given attention to God's Word before an attack, the battle will be harder because you entered the fight weak.

Even if you've become strong by doing all the above, you can lose respect for your foundation and be tempted to choose another. That's why you must keep your guard up and not get distracted by life's cares: "Therefore we must give the more earnest heed to the things we have heard, lest we drift away. For if the word spoken through angels proved steadfast, and every transgression and disobedience received a just reward, how shall we escape if we neglect so great a salvation, which at the first began to be spoken by the Lord, and was confirmed to us by those who heard Him…" (Hebrews 2:1-3) No matter what the season in your life may be, consistently do the above points as a *lifestyle*, so your faith stays stable and continues to grow. If your confidence begins to shift, you are more easy prey for the devil. He will find your weakness and attempt to steal that Word from you.

Matthew 13:18-23 is the well-known Parable of the Sower. It tells of a sower who scattered the seed of God's Word on the soil, or hearts, of four people.

Following the parable, Jesus explains it so His disciples could understand:

> "Listen then to the [meaning of the] parable of the sower: When anyone hears the word of the kingdom [regarding salvation] and does not understand and grasp it, the evil one comes and snatches away what was sown in his heart. This is the one on whom seed was sown beside the road. The one on whom seed was sown on rocky ground, this is the one who hears the word and at once welcomes it with joy; yet he has no [substantial] root in himself, but is only temporary, and when pressure or persecution comes because of the word, immediately he stumbles and falls away [abandoning the One who is the source of salvation]. And the one on whom seed was sown among thorns, this is the one who hears the word, but the worries and distractions of the world and the deceitfulness [the superficial pleasures and delight] of riches choke the word, and it yields no fruit. And the one on whom seed was sown on the good soil, this is the one who hears the word and understands and grasps it; he indeed bears fruit and yields, some a hundred times [as much as was sown], some sixty [times as much], and some thirty" (Mathew 13:18-23, AMP).

Notice each of these people had the same Word preached to them, yet each responded differently. Each had a strength or weakness that caused the Word to die or caused it to grow.

THE WAYSIDE SOIL

The first example describes a person who does not understand the Word that is given to them. They hear it but it goes in one ear and out the other. The Word falls to the wayside where it is easy for the devil to come and snatch away. Because they didn't diligently guard their heart and seek to understand, the Word doesn't produce anything in their lives (Proverbs 4:23).

THE STONY SOIL

The second example talks about someone who gets excited about the Word, but the joy is shallow and temporary, more based on emotion. They don't value it enough to study it and get it into their heart. As a result, it becomes head knowledge rather than a firm conviction of the Word's truth, and the trials of life quickly overcome them. Again, nothing comes from the Word's planting.

THE THORNY SOIL

The third example tells of someone who hears the Word, but it doesn't bear any fruit because other things come in and snuff out its potential. Life, with all its allurements and cares, is a higher priority to this person. Like the stony soil, they don't value the Word enough to give it their attention. Their life then holds no godly fruit.

THE GOOD SOIL

The fourth example was much different than the first three. It describes good soil—someone who both hears the Word and understands it. They can understand it because they value it and allow it to go deep into their heart. They become rooted and grounded in what they believe, rather than letting the devil, distractions, and the cares of life to overcome it (Colossians 2:7). The result? They produce fruit.

Notice that the sower did not force the soil to be good soil. He simply sowed the Word. Just the same, God does not decide for you what soil you will be. You have the power to understand and to see it produce in your life. But you must value and be receptive to the Word you're given for it to bear fruit. You can either allow life and its distractions to influence your heart, or you can value God's Word enough to study it, speak it, and act on it (Proverbs 4:20). How much you do this determines how much fruit you will produce. It's *your* choice.

> And the disciples came and said to Him, "Why do You speak to them in parables?" He answered and said to them, "Because it has been given to you to know the mysteries of the kingdom of heaven, but to them it has not been given. For whoever has, to him more will be given, and he will have abundance; but whoever does not have, even what he has will be taken away from him. Therefore I

speak to them in parables, because seeing they do not see, and hearing they do not hear, nor do they understand" (Matthew 13:10-13).

The Bible states that you can know people by the fruit they bear in their lives (Matthew 7:15-20). If you want to project God's nature in your life, you must have good soil that produces good trees that produce good fruit. Good fruit would include a holy lifestyle, answered prayer, love and good works, and a faithfulness to the Kingdom of God. This is the fruit of a victorious life. As you produce this fruit, refuse to be moved from your foundation. As Ephesians 6 in the Amplified Classic says "hold your ground" and "stand firmly in place." You will not be moved!

> He only is my rock and my salvation; He is my defense; I shall not be greatly moved (Psalm 62:2).

> …except that the Holy Spirit testifies in every city, saying that chains and tribulations await me. But none of these things move me; nor do I count my life dear to myself, so that I may finish my race with joy, and the ministry which I received from the Lord Jesus, to testify to the gospel of the grace of God (Acts 20:23-24).

CHAPTER 4

YOU STAND BY FAITH

OFTEN, WHEN YOU hear the word "faith," you may think it is something only possessed by the spiritual elite like pastors or traveling ministers. On the contrary, you have faith because God placed it in your heart when you were saved (Romans 12:3). Faith is simply believing, or having a solid persuasion or conviction, that something is true. God knew you needed it to live a victoriously in life. You can't please Him or receive anything from Him without it.

> "But without faith it is impossible to please Him, for he who comes to God must believe that He is, and that He is a rewarder of those who diligently seek Him" (Hebrews 11:6).

> Now He did not do many mighty works there because of their unbelief (Matthew 3:58).

Even your salvation was a result of faith. You believed that Jesus was the Son of God and declared Him as the Lord of your life (Ephesians 2:8-9; Romans 10:9-10). It was simple—and had everything to do with believing and trusting from the heart—including in your battles.

> "Not that we have dominion over your faith, but are fellow workers for your joy; for by faith you stand" (2 Corinthians 1:24).

> Now faith is the assurance (the confirmation, the title deed) of the things [we] hope for, being the proof of things [we] do not see and the conviction of their reality [faith perceiving as real fact what is not revealed to the senses] (Hebrews 11:1, AMPC).

It's important to know that true faith does not involve "trying." Trying includes doubt that something will work. You try on clothes at a store because you're uncertain that they will fit. You try a new hairdresser to give them chance to prove themselves. You try a new recipe, unsure that it will taste good. True faith, however, is confident that what God says, He will do. It does not hope in the world's form of hope—just wishful desire that something will happen. Instead, it has biblical hope—confident expectation—which contains no doubt or uncertainty. It knows without a doubt because it knows the nature of God is faithful, and all His promises are a resounding "yes and amen" (2 Corinthians 1:20)!

EXAMPLES OF VICTORY THROUGH FAITH

Israel was a nation that had to learn to stand to get the victory over their enemies. Sometimes they obeyed God's commands and got the victory. Other times they blatantly disobeyed God and turned toward other gods, resulting in their defeat and captivity. But the times they chose to follow God's instructions resulted in their success.

Let's look at a couple examples from the Old Testament. The first is when they were between the Red Sea and the Egyptians:

> And Moses said to the people, "Do not be afraid. Stand still, and see the salvation of the LORD, which He will accomplish for you today. For the Egyptians whom you see today, you shall see again no more forever. The LORD will fight for you, and you shall hold your peace." And the LORD said to Moses, "Why do you cry to Me? Tell the children of Israel to go forward. But lift up your rod, and stretch out your hand over the sea and divide it. And the children of Israel shall go on dry ground through the midst of the sea. And I indeed will harden the hearts of the Egyptians, and they shall follow them. So I will gain honor over Pharaoh and over all his army, his chariots, and his horsemen. Then the Egyptians shall know that I am the LORD, when I have gained honor for Myself over Pharaoh, his chariots, and his horsemen" (Exodus 14:13-18).

Another example from the Old Testament is when Moab and Ammon came against Israel under the reign of King Jehoshaphat. After the king and the people prayed and fasted, God spoke through a Levite named Jahaziel these words:

> And he said, "Listen, all you of Judah and you inhabitants of Jerusalem, and you, King Jehoshaphat! Thus says the Lord to you: 'Do not be afraid nor dismayed because of this great multitude, for the battle is not yours, but God's. Tomorrow go down against them. They will surely come up by the Ascent of Ziz, and you will find them at the end of the brook before the Wilderness of Jeruel. You will not need to fight in this battle. Position yourselves, stand still and see the salvation of the Lord, who is with you, O Judah and Jerusalem!' Do not fear or be dismayed; tomorrow go out against them, for the Lord is with you" (2 Chronicles 20:15-17).

Notice that God took this attack against Israel personally. He declared that it was *His* battle, not theirs. When the devil attacks you, God takes it personally—and personally defends you. But you need to cooperate with God by following simple commands. These are all biblical principles—guidelines for fighting any spiritual battle. Faith is timeless. It never changes.

WHAT FAITH DOES

FAITH SEEKS GOD FIRST

People who reject Jesus choose to seek after the world's system rather than after God. They do not honor God and think they can manage without Him. They believe that people and their efforts will get them what they want and need (Psalm 10:4). As a result of relying on themselves, they choose the devil's way: leaning on their own understanding. They try to figure things out on their own without consulting God. It often comes in the form of looking to doctors as their primary source of healing; trying to make money in whatever way they can; and looking to the government to take care of them, etc.

God, on the other hand, has commanded you to trust in Him above your own intellect and power (Proverbs 3:5-6). He has called you to seek Him *first*: "But seek first the kingdom of God and His righteousness, and all these things shall be added to you" (Matthew 6:33). When you put God first, seeking Him first as your main source of provision, He will honor you with all that you need. Failure to seek Him leads to defeat.

A good example of this is King Asa in 2 Chronicles 14-16. King Asa honored God by destroying the false gods in the land of Israel and leading the country back to God. God then honored him with victory over his enemies. However, there came a time when King Asa did not consult God concerning a pending battle but joined himself with a pagan country to deliver them. The result? It was prophesied that Israel would lose its peace and continue to have war. He didn't seem to learn his lesson because shortly after he became ill, he sought after medical doctors alone rather than after God first for a solution. He died of a disease in his feet as a result.

Is it wrong to utilize natural means? No. God uses natural means such as doctors to help you. What is wrong is when your trust is in the natural and you don't seek after God *first*. This is an indication that you have more faith in people and natural solutions than you do in God. God will not respond with His help if He takes second place. He's looking for someone who will obey, trust, and seek in Him with a whole heart (Psalm 119:2-3). Once you've sought His will and insight, He may choose to utilize something in the natural. But it will be by His design, not yours, and His grace will be on it as you follow His instructions (Psalm 34:10, Hebrews 11:6).

FAITH HEARS FROM GOD

Romans 8:17 says, "So then faith comes by hearing, and hearing by the word of God." Before you can have faith for something, you must have a word from God. You must know His will—His Word—before you can believe Him and act on what He said, whether it's a Scripture or a word spoken to your heart. This is exactly what Israel did. They heard God's instruction, which gave them something to believe. And because they trusted His trustworthy nature, they were confident to act on what He said.

FAITH PRAYS

Prayer is the first step to receiving anything from God. He, of course, knows your needs. He can read your thoughts, but He will not force His blessings on you. He expects you to ask because you are confident in His love for you and His desire for victory in your life. He's delighted when you take Him at His Word!

> Now this is the confidence that we have in Him, that if we ask anything according to His will, He hears us. And if we know that He hears us, whatever we ask, we know that we have the petitions that we have asked of Him (1 John 5:14-15).
>
> Until now you have asked nothing in My name. Ask, and you will receive, that your joy may be full (John 16:24).
>
> Therefore I say to you, whatever things you ask when you pray, believe that you receive them, and you will have them (Mark 11:24).

According to 1 John 5:14-15, you received your promise the moment you prayed. From that moment on, you can stand on those Scriptures without giving up, no matter how long it takes for the answer to appear. You have, after all, God's Word on it. It's not a useless, inactive Word. You can expect it to produce results.

FAITH STANDS STILL

God's second command to Israel was to stand still. This almost seems to contradict "faith without works is dead" (James 2:20). But God did require them to act, just not by fighting physically. This corresponds with Ephesians 6:12:

> For we do not wrestle against flesh and blood, but against principalities, against powers, against the rulers of the darkness of this age, against spiritual hosts of wickedness in the heavenly places.

Your enemies are not people or organizations. Your enemy is the devil. If you were to start fighting people physically or verbally, the result would not be victory. The root of every problem, conflict, stress, or harassment is the devil. He must be dealt with first through the Word by using your God-given authority (more on this in a next chapter). If there is some discussion or legal action that needs to be taken, it should always be done in love, submitted to God, and bathed in prayer. No matter what, always remember that the devil—not a person—is at the root of it all.

FAITH IS FEARLESS

The first command God gave Israel was not to fear. Fear is the enemy and complete opposite of faith. It does not come from God.

"For God has not given us a spirit of fear, but of power and of love and of a sound mind" (2 Timothy 1:7).

While faith is confidence that God's Word is true and that He will do what He says, fear is uncertainty that God will do what He says. Fear is not trusting God and puts more confidence in the enemy than in God and His Word (more on this in a future chapter). It is not trusting God, so it cancels out your faith—your believing—and hinders God from working on your behalf (i.e. the children of Israel feared, resulting in God postponing their entrance into the Promised Land).

FAITH ACTS ON WHAT IT BELIEVES

God requires action when it comes to operating in faith. Israel followed God's instructions to get dressed and put on their sandals in preparation for departure from Egypt, even while they were still slaves. In Chronicles, He told them to begin walking toward the enemy camp while worshiping despite the size of their enemy. They marched around the Jericho and shouted, even though naturally no wall could fall by that method. David picked out stones for his sling, regardless of Goliath's towering image. Mary's friends poured water into wine pots despite how crazy it seemed. Thankfully, none of these people acted on their fears, but acted on their faith in God. They were all delivered and had their problems solved by believing and acting on that what God said.

Take a moment to read Hebrews 11. It's what is considered the "Great Hall of Faith" because it describes what great men and women of faith did in response to what they believed. Many verses begin with "by faith" and tells what they did. Victory, blessings, and a good report from God followed their actions.

The Bible makes it clear that people who receive from God are those who believe and don't doubt. That confidence doesn't sit dormant inside someone's heart. Action follows. We might think there was something wrong with a farmer if he called himself a farmer but never went out into his field and planted seed. We'd really be concerned if one of our friends announced they were an employee at the mall yet never got off the couch to work for a paycheck. The Bible says in James 2:14-17 (AMPC) that faith without works is dead:

> What is the benefit, my fellow believers, if someone claims to have faith but has no [good] works [as evidence]? Can that [kind of] faith save him? [No, a mere claim of faith is not sufficient—genuine faith produces good works.] If a brother or sister is without [adequate] clothing and lacks [enough] food for each day, and one of you says to them, "Go in peace [with my blessing], [keep] warm and feed yourselves," but he does not give them the necessities for the body, what good does that do? So too, faith, if it does not have works [to back it up], is by itself dead [inoperative and ineffective].

God may tell you to participate in something that you physically can't feel up to doing. He may tell you to show acts of kindness even though your relationship doesn't seem salvageable. He may tell you to praise when life's circumstances are weighing you down. He may tell you to give financially to your church or to someone in need even though your own finances are tight.

Years ago, the devil attacked me with a sickness that left me physically weak after recovery. As staff at my church, I was asked to help at your church's kid's camp. It required leading a group of children from one activity to the next, sometimes out in the summer heat. Before the camp began, I helped deliver food to houses where camp staff would be staying. Even when doing this I felt very weak. As I sat in the van's driver's seat, I asked God how I was going to be able to endure the following week's activities. He spoke to my heart clearly, "Move forward confidently, doubting nothing." I took Him at His Word and entered the camp week, trusting that He would give me the strength I needed. Sure enough, I ran and jumped with the twelve children assigned to me—in the heat—with no negative symptoms. I even housed teenage girls at my trailer, which included late nights. If I had not "moved forward confidently, doubting nothing," I am confident I would have not had the strength and health God had promised. God required *me* to act on what He said to see His promise fulfilled.

Often, people decide for themselves what their faith action should be. True faith, however, always acts on a

Word from God, not an assumption. Nor does it copy someone else's faith action. Just because someone runs a marathon while ill doesn't mean you should. Just because someone gives away *all* their money to gain a financial harvest for their financial need, doesn't mean you should do the same. Your faith must be genuine—from your *own* heart and from your *own* word from God. Otherwise, it's fake, or pretend faith, which could cost you your victory (2 Timothy 1:5). Whatever He tells *you* to do, do it (John 2:5). That's where your victory lies!

FAITH IS NOT MOVED BY WHAT IT SEES

Years ago, sonograms didn't exist. It was rarely used, and only for emergencies. The pleasure of knowing the gender of your baby or seeing the accurate growth of organs wasn't possible. The only proof of a pregnancy was physical symptoms, a growing tummy, and movement in the womb.

Could you imagine a woman who had an "I'll believe it when I see it" attitude when she first felt signs of pregnancy? "Yes, I know my stomach is getting big and the doctor says I'm pregnant. But I don't *see* a baby so I can't believe it's actually there." You would find this attitude ridiculous!

Sadly, some people treat God's promises much the same way. When God's Word says "by Jesus stripes you're healed" (Isaiah 53:5), they wait for symptoms to improve to believe it. When God promises to supply all their needs, they watch the bank account to determine whether it's true (Philippians 4:19). When they pray for protection, they cower behind closed doors, unwilling to live as if God would do what He said He would do in Psalm 91. It's as if they're waiting on a "sonogram" to determine what they believe.

This is completely opposite of what faith really looks like. Faith doesn't believe because it's *sees*. Faith believes *regardless* of what it sees.

> "For we walk by faith, not by sight" (2 Corinthians 5:7).

True faith doesn't depend on the visual to believe. You weren't there when Jesus died on the cross, yet you believe that you're saved because you received Jesus as your Lord and Savior. You haven't seen heaven, yet you believe you are going there one day. You read Bible stories and consider them as factual. Why then is it so challenging to believe for things far less significant than eternal salvation? The answer is that your body and emotions often become so accustomed—especially in this culture—to placing your day-to-day confidence in what you *physically* see rather than placing it in God's *spiritual* reality.

> For our momentary, light distress [this passing trouble] is producing for us an eternal weight of glory [a fullness] beyond all measure [surpassing all comparisons, a transcendent splendor and an endless blessedness]! So we look not at the

things which are seen, but at the things which are unseen; for the things which are visible are temporal [just brief and fleeting], but the things which are invisible are everlasting *and* imperishable (2 Corinthians 4:17-18, AMP).

God is a spiritual being, and everything He says and does starts in the spiritual realm. When He says something, it's as real as if it manifested in the natural realm immediately for your eyes to see. He doesn't think, "Maybe what I just said will come to pass … but then maybe it won't." The moment He declared it, it was so, even if your physical eyes could not see it right away. Like God's faith in His own Word, your faith must be in His unfailing supernatural Word before you see it. This determines what you receive in the natural. You must forget about the "sonograms" and wholly trust in His Word. God doesn't operate any other way.

Blessed are those who have not seen and yet have believed (John 20:29b).

FAITH SPEAKS ONLY GOD'S WORD

As Isaiah 55 says, God's Word in your mouth is just as powerful as it is in His. He has called you to speak what He has said in His Word with the expectation that it will accomplish His purpose. Never discount what He has said, claiming that it is old and out of date. Instead, confidently believe that His Word is true. Out of that belief comes your confident repeating what He said.

He won't force you to speak His Word, however. He has given you the ability to choose between saying what He says or saying what the devil says. The one you choose will determine whether you receive life or death (Proverbs 18:21). It guides the course of your life, whether you arrive safely at your harbor of victory, or get shipwrecked on the island of defeat. You will have the things you say, so choose your words wisely.

> Indeed, we put bits in horses' mouths that they may obey us, and we turn their whole body. Look also at ships: although they are so large and are driven by fierce winds, they are turned by a very small rudder wherever the pilot desires. Even so the tongue is a little member and boasts great things. See how great a forest a little fire kindles! (James 3:3-5).

> You will also declare a thing, and it will be established for you; so light will shine on your ways (Job 22:28).

> "A good man out of the good treasure of his heart brings forth good things, and an evil man out of the evil treasure brings forth evil things. But I say to you that for every idle word men may speak, they will give account of it in the day of judgment. For by your words you will be justified, and by your words you will be condemned" (Matthew 12:35-37).

God changed Abram's name (meaning exalted father) to Abraham (father of many nations) as a sign of God's promise of a child. From that day forward, Abraham repeated God's promise with his mouth, even though there was no child for his physical eyes to see. He followed God's example and called those things that "be not as though they were," the same action He took when speaking the world into existence (Romans 4:17, Hebrews 11:3). God wants you to not only believe, but speak what you believe, not what you feel or see (2 Corinthians 4:13).

Luke 6:45b says, "For out of the abundance of the heart his mouth speaks." What comes out of your mouth indicates what's on the inside of you—faith or doubt. Regardless of how you feel or what's going on around you, God wants you to "hold fast the profession of your faith without wavering" (Hebrews 10:23). Your "profession" is also translated "confession." "Of your faith" states what you believe. To confess means to say the same thing as. You are to say exactly what God says, lining up your words with His to see positive results. Saying anything less turns into an idle word, or a curse, that does not bless your situation.

The devil thrives on idle words even though you may not mean them literally (i.e. "That just kills me!" or "I'm sicker than a dog!"). He also notes the words you say that do not have faith attached to them. Faith is the key to making your God-words work. It's possible to confess God's Word, yet not see results, simply because you didn't believe they would make a difference. You can go through the motions of speaking them each day, but a doubt-free, believing heart is what it takes to receive God's promises.

The devil does not want you to receive God's promises. But since *he* can't stop your heart from believing, he will bombard your mind with negative thoughts to distract you. These thoughts may contain doubts, fears, anxiety, or even anger. Then he'll tempt you to speak those negative thoughts.

Instead of receiving and speaking those negative thoughts, a heart trusting in God throws them out (2 Corinthians 10:5). Instead, it says things like, "Thank God He is for me and not against me," "I am more than a conquer because He loves me," or "I have the victory in this battle." They aren't words of discouragement; they are words of confidence. Those are the words God is waiting to hear! He loves it when you identify with His promise by declaring every day what He says—even when you don't see the victory with your physical eyes.

FAITH RECEIVES THE VICTORY

Notice the examples in Hebrews 11 did not end in defeat; they ended in victory. Those who didn't seem to receive the victory were those who chose to lay down their lives for the Kingdom of God so they could receive a greater reward. But those who stood against enemies and hardship received the promise of deliverance. This is also true of the children of Israel in 2 Chronicles 20 and Exodus

20. Their faith produced the victory, just as 1 John 5:4 declares: "For whatever is born of God overcomes the world. And this is the victory that has overcome the world—our faith." You can confidently expect the same!

(Please see "The Characteristics of Those Who Live by Faith" in the Resources section at the end of book.)

CHAPTER 5

YOU STAND WITH CHRIST'S AUTHORITY

SIMPLY PUT, AUTHORITY is the power to take charge and create change. Like it or not, it always has been and always will be in existence, starting with God. He is the one and only true God and reigns over all (Isaiah 45:5, Psalm 103:19). He exercised His authority in heaven as He reigned over the angels and spiritual beings. He exercised His authority when He kicked Satan out of heaven (Revelation 12:7-9). Then, when He created Adam and Eve, He gave them dominion, or authority over the Garden He made for them.

> Then God said, "Let Us make man in Our image, according to Our likeness; let them have dominion over the fish of the sea, over the birds of the air, and over the cattle, over all the earth and over every

creeping thing that creeps on the earth." So God created man in His *own* image; in the image of God He created him; male and female He created them. Then God blessed them, and God said to them, "Be fruitful and multiply; fill the earth and subdue it; have dominion over the fish of the sea, over the birds of the air, and over every living thing that moves on the earth" (Genesis 1:26-28).

Unfortunately, Adam and Eve gave up that authority and allowed Satan to be in charge (2 Corinthians 4:4, Luke 4:6, Romans 5:17). Not until Jesus came to earth was the authority given back to His people.

> "Behold! I have given you authority *and* power to trample upon serpents and scorpions, and [physical and mental strength and ability] over all the power that the enemy [possesses]; and nothing shall in any way harm you" (Luke 10:19, AMP).

Mark 16:15-18 gets specific:

> "And He said to them, "Go into all the world and preach the gospel to every creature. He who believes and is baptized will be saved; but he who does not believe will be condemned. And these signs will follow those who believe: In My name they will cast out demons; they will speak with new tongues; they will take up serpents; and if they drink anything deadly, it will by no means hurt them; they will lay hands on the sick, and they will recover."

Your authority is over the devil and his works. You do not have power over people, except through civil law (also ordained by God). To try to exercise authority over people in any other area is misused authority. It's not backed by a higher authority.

For instance, your authority over the devil and his works is like that of a police officer whose badge carries weight wherever he goes. Though the badge doesn't hold any power by itself, the authority of the police department behind that piece of metal proclaims a police officer's right to give commands. Just the same, without the power of God backing you up, your words against the devil would fall to the ground, harmless. On your own, you couldn't get the tiniest ant to do what you commanded, much less a spiritual demon. That's why you need to consistently stay submitted to your Police Chief, Jesus. James 4:7 says, "Submit yourselves therefore to God. Resist the devil, and he will flee from you."

Your position of submission to God's leadership keeps you in line with His blessings and the authority that belongs to you. No power can flow unless you're living with God as your head. Jewish exorcists found this out the hard way in the book of Acts:

> Now God worked unusual miracles by the hands of Paul, so that even handkerchiefs or aprons were brought from his body to the sick, and the diseases left them and the evil spirits went out of them. Then some of the itinerant Jewish exorcists took it upon themselves to call the name of the Lord

Jesus over those who had evil spirits, saying, "We exorcise you by the Jesus whom Paul preaches." Also, there were seven sons of Sceva, a Jewish chief priest, who did so. And the evil spirit answered and said, "Jesus I know, and Paul I know; but who are you?" Then the man in whom the evil spirit was leaped on them, overpowered them, and prevailed against them, so that they fled out of that house naked and wounded. This became known both to all Jews and Greeks dwelling in Ephesus; and fear fell on them all, and the name of the Lord Jesus was magnified (Acts 19:11-19).

The devil recognizes rebellion. He knows who's on God's side and who's not. He has no fear when he can see God's power is not in your favor. He will do anything to distract you from your allegiance to God by sending darts of doubt and rebellion that may come in the form of:

- Disobedience to God's Word and the plan of God for your life
- Unforgiveness toward others
- Weak faith due to time not spent in His Word
- Inability to hear God's voice due to life's constant distractions

Like in the instance of Ananias and Sapphira in Acts 5:1-10, sin can open the door for judgement from God. Ananias and Sapphira lied to the disciples and the Holy

Spirit about the amount of offering they were to give. As a result, both people fell dead.

As we discussed before, one of God's titles is Righteous Judge (Psalm 7:11). There are passages in the Bible that indicate He allowed or issued acts of judgement on evil and evil doers. He does not, however, inflict pain or death to His children. But when He lifts His hand of protection off someone due to disobedience, it opens the door for the devil to gain entrance to that person's life. Though you may not always experience physical death upon sinning, giving entrance to the devil is serious. It could result in unanswered prayer, sickness, strife in relationships, financial ruin, loss of a job—the list goes on. It's your responsibility to stay undistracted enough to keep your badge glowing and your gun loaded. When you keep your own ammunition employed, you can stand with confidence, expecting results!

POWER IN THE NAME

SPEAK THE NAME

Along with that right of authority is the power of a weapon—the name of Jesus. The use of Jesus's name is the same as that of a police officer pointing his gun at a vandal and telling him to stop. Power is contained in that gun and the hand holding it.

Amarillo, Texas, had just been buffeted with a rare ice storm, leaving the streets slippery and glass-like. Traffic was slow on the smaller, residential streets, but as I got onto the interstate, everyone seemed immune to the recent weather change. They flew by with regular speed, anxious to get to work on time like I was. Though a few cars sped passed me like their tails were on fire, I maintained a slightly slower pace. But it wasn't slow enough. Suddenly, my blue Ford Explorer hit black ice, and I spun out of control. No amount of frantic hand or foot work would slow my crazy plunge toward the overpass railing—my only barrier between me and the access road below. All I could do was scream, "*JESUS!*"

As quickly as I had lost control, I came to a screeching halt in front of the railing. My heart pounding, I got out to examine my predicament. To my amazement, my Explorer's bumper wasn't even touching the railing. It was just inches from it! No scratches, no dents. Just proof that something greater than ice had stopped my impending descent to the street beneath me.

I have no doubt that my desperate cry for deliverance in the Name of Jesus had saved me from going over the railing that day. Under normal circumstances, an accident between me and another oncoming car was more than likely. But no railing or oncoming car was a match for the power of Jesus's Name that day. Psalm 91:14 says, "Because he has set his love upon Me, therefore I will deliver him; I will set him on high because he has *known My name*" (italics added).

COMMAND IN THE NAME

The key is to understand and respect His name and speak it. If there is a problem in your life that needs to be removed, it's your responsibility to *command*—not ask or nag—for it to go. You can know His Name yet not exercise your authority in it.

It was a quiet Saturday afternoon as I cuddled up with my Bible in my tiny second-story apartment living room. Quiet, until I heard heavy footsteps outside on the porch that joined my apartment to my neighbor's. Two male voices proceeded to carry on an animated conversation outside my front door.

Frowning, I went to the peep hole in my door and looked out. Two men, probably in their mid to late twenties, stood just outside my door, leaning against the porch railing. *My* porch railing. They were tall and muscular and bore tattoos on their arms. One man spoke quietly. The other, however, appeared to be drunk as he loudly began to rant and rave about the latest aggravation in his life. If having two complete male strangers on *my* front porch wasn't enough, the talkative one decided the "F" word was appropriate to use every other word he said.

Irritated, I went back to my couch. I was too intimidated by their size and gender to open the door. Instead, I tried to resume my Bible-reading, hoping they'd eventually disappear. No such luck. They remained on the porch, the mouthy one still spouting off profanities.

Now I was getting mad. I was trying to read my

Bible, and all I could hear was a drunken bad attitude strewn with the "F" bomb.

I resorted to prayer: "God, I pray that those men would leave my front porch!"

Nothing happened.

My agitation growing, I jumped to my feet. "In the Name of Jesus, I command the spirit of profanity to leave my porch!"

Nothing.

Finally, I'd had enough of those mouthy trespassers. I swung open the door with sudden confidence. The two men spun around, their eyes wide with surprise. "I can hear every word you're saying," I spouted, "and I don't appreciate hearing that kind of language." They began to back off my porch like whipped puppies. "Oh, sorry, ma'am," the calmer one stuttered. "We were just trying to get out of the sun." With those final words, they hurried down the steps and down the street.

I shut the door and returned to my couch and my Bible, rejoicing in my victory. What amazed me was that my five-foot-two, one-hundred-pound body could intimidate two men three times my size. I didn't even look my age, yet one open door and one word of correction was enough to send them sheepishly on their way.

I would *never* recommend that a woman open her

door to male strangers. But in this case, God was teaching me something. This experience reminded me of another enemy that often stands at your door, wanting more than to chat. He comes to harass and annoy, steal, kill, and destroy (John 10:10). Yet, like I did in the beginning, it's tempting to stand timidly behind the closed door, only wishing he'd go away. You may even pray to God for some assistance when God expects you to confront him.

> I assure you *and* most solemnly say to you, whoever says to this mountain, 'Be lifted up and thrown into the sea!' and does not doubt in his heart [in God's unlimited power], but believes that what he says is going to take place, it will be done for him [in accordance with God's will]. For this reason I am telling you, whatever things you ask for in prayer [in accordance with God's will], believe [with confident trust] that you have received them, and they will be *given* to you (Mark 11:23-24, AMPC).

There's no telling how long those strangers would have stayed on my front porch had I not decided to open my front door. It could have been hours perhaps had I not been willing to face them. Those two men on the porch needed to see *my* face. They needed to know that they weren't welcome on *my* porch. They needed to hear *my* voice. Once I decided I'd had enough and acted on my authority, it gave them reason to leave.

This is what God expects of you as well. He doesn't

want you running to Him in faithless panic like the children of Israel did when they encountered giants in the land. Though He loves you deeply and cares about what you're going through, He is not pleased when He hears whining (Philippians 2:14; Jude 1:14-19; Philippians 4:11-13). Consider, for instance, what happened when the children of Israel complained about the manna or the giants in the land. They suffered hardship and didn't receive their promised land. Instead of following their example, God requires that you to rise and use the authority He gave you over Satan, facing him head-on with confidence and strength like the apostles did in the Book of Acts. This is the only way to victory!

> Now Peter and John went up together to the temple at the hour of prayer, the ninth hour. And a certain man lame from his mother's womb was carried, whom they laid daily at the gate of the temple which is called Beautiful, to ask alms from those who entered the temple; who, seeing Peter and John about to go into the temple, asked for alms. And fixing his eyes on him, with John, Peter said, "Look at us." So he gave them his attention, expecting to receive something from them. Then Peter said, "Silver and gold I do not have, but what I do have I give you: *In the name of Jesus Christ of Nazareth*, rise up and walk." And he took him by the right hand and lifted him up, and immediately his feet and ankle bones received strength. So he,

leaping up, stood and walked and entered the temple with them—walking, leaping, and praising God (Acts 3:1-8, italics added).

HAVE CONFIDENCE IN THE NAME

"But what if I don't see my mountain move right away?" you might ask.

If you look at what you can see with your physical eyes, it's easy to get discouraged. Like true faith does, you must maintain your confidence in the Name you just spoke to see any results. Faith doesn't look at what is going on in the natural, physical realm. It stays confident in God's Word, regardless of what it sees.

Let's consider Jesus's example in Mark 11:12-25. Jesus and his disciples were traveling and were hungry. Seeing a fig tree, Jesus went to it, hopeful for a bite to eat. Instead, He found nothing but leaves. His response? "Let no one eat fruit from you ever again" (verse 12). Then the next morning when they walked by, they found that the fig tree had dried up at its roots. Note that it took time to see the results from Jesus's command. The tree didn't whither the moment Jesus spoke—at least not for their eyes to see. The death of the tree started at the root before it appeared on the limbs and leaves for anyone to notice. It's then in verse 22 that Jesus exhorted His disciples to speak to the mountain, the problem. Note He said to do it without doubting, confident that it would move. Those who speak with authority will "have whatever he says."

Never give up if nothing seems to happen when you command your problem to move in Jesus Name. Something *is* happening in the spiritual realm. The devil and his influences are moving, loosening their hold on your situation. At any moment, the mountain could be gone for everyone around you to see!

God's nature and the Great Commission has not changed (Malachi 3:6, Numbers 23:19, Hebrews 13:8). The same authority exercised by the Apostles is still in effect today. Don't just quietly sit by and wait for something to change. Stay alert while standing in your armor so you are quick to perceive when the devil is trying to override the authority you hold. You *will* see your mountain move!

> Be sober, be vigilant; because your adversary the devil walks about like a roaring lion, seeking whom he may devour (1 Peter 5:8).

CHAPTER 6

YOU STAND WITHOUT FEAR

THE WORLD HOLDS many reasons to fear—sickness, severe weather, violence, and poverty, just to name a few. You may have experienced one or more of these. More than likely, fear was an automatic symptom that accompanied the event.

Second Timothy 1:7 clearly states that God is not the author of fear: "For God has not given us a spirit of fear, but of power and of love and of a sound mind." If fear doesn't come from Him, then where does fear come from?

According to God's Word, fear is from the devil. Just like sin came into the world when Adam and Eve disobeyed, fear entered the world when the devil was given rule of the earth. One of the first negative emotions that Adam and Eve experienced was fear. The moment God called, they hid themselves, afraid of being found in their naked, sinful state (Genesis 3:8). They received a package that was not from God and acted on it.

Fear is a negative emotion based on thoughts inspired by negative events that may or may not happen. It is the opposite of faith in God. It is faith in evil, believing that something negative could happen. You can identify fear by comparing the negative, fearful thoughts to the Bible's description of God, the devil, and their natures. If the thought is pure and good, it's from God the Father (1 John 1:5). But if it's negative and evil, it comes straight from Satan (John 10:10).

So, when you have a negative, fearful thought of any kind come to mind, ask yourself the following questions and compare it to these Scripture verses:

- Is it negative (Philippians 4:8)?
- Does it bring torment (1 John 4:18a)?
- Does it violate the plan of God for my life (Jeremiah 29:11)?
- Does it inspire me to commit the sin of worry (Matthew 6:25)?

If you can say "yes" to any of those four points above, you can determine that these thoughts and feelings are not from God. From there you have the choice to receive or reject them. God, as the God of peace, has instructed you to reject them: "Fear not, for I am with you; be not dismayed, for I am your God. I will strengthen you, yes, I will help you, I will uphold you with My righteous right hand" (Isaiah 41:10).

Notice that fear always results in the stress that something isn't going to turn out in your favor, that something is going to harm you (1 John 4:18). Stress of any kind does not come from God. He is a God of peace and doesn't want your life controlled by fear (1 Thessalonians 5:23, Philippians 4:9). It robs you of the peace He gives and destroys your faith in Him. It harms you emotionally, physically, and spiritually. It undermines your health, inspires irrational thinking, and triggers bad decision-making. It hinders you from receiving good things from God, and allows the devil to steal, kill, and destroy you. Most of all, fear intimidates and hampers you from influencing people for good and doing God's will on the earth. The devil doesn't want you to enjoy a life of peace; and he especially doesn't want you to advance the Kingdom of God. If you were unshackled from *all* fear, you would be unstoppable!

Often, you may think of fear in connection with something like a cancer diagnosis or weathering a looming hurricane. But fear also comes in more subtle forms such as worry, nervousness, shyness, phobias, and even indecisiveness. But regardless of the size, God wants you to deal with the fear, leaving it behind for good. No matter how great the problem seems to you, He doesn't consider one issue as more difficult to resolve than the other. They are all "care packages" sent from the devil. Instead of receiving those packages, choose to cast them all on Him: "Casting all your care upon him; for he cares for you" (I Peter 5:7). It is possible to live fearless when you believe and trust a God with whom all things are possible (Matthew 19:26, Mark 9:23)!

TRUST FEARLESSLY

Feeding your body and wearing clothes is a necessity of life. In fact, it would be the first two basic material things that you couldn't live without. Jesus knew the importance of these, yet He made it clear in Luke 12:22-23 that life is more than these things: "Then He said to His disciples, 'Therefore I say to you, do not worry about your life, what you will eat; nor about the body, what you will put on. Life is more than food, and the body is more than clothing.'"

When you consider how you couldn't survive without food, and would surely die in some climates without clothes, hearing these words almost sounds unrealistic and insensitive. But Jesus is clear that you, not the food you eat or the clothes you wear, determine the value of your life. Your value comes from your status as a spiritual being with a spiritual purpose on this earth (Genesis 1:27). As a result, you are of greater value than the flowers ... and the birds. This being the case, God has promised to provide for you, just as He promised to provide for them.

> Consider the ravens, for they neither sow nor reap, which have neither storehouse nor barn; and God feeds them. Of how much more value are you than the birds? And which of you by worrying can add

one cubit to his stature? If you then are not able to do the least, why are you anxious for the rest? Consider the lilies, how they grow: they neither toil nor spin; and yet I say to you, even Solomon in all his glory was not arrayed like one of these. If then God so clothes the grass, which today is in the field and tomorrow is thrown into the oven, how much more will He clothe you, O you of little faith (Luke 12:24-28?).

God, as your Father through the sacrifice of Jesus, has committed Himself to take care of you. That care comes from His heart of love, the reason you have no reason to fear. That love for you has the power to cast out all fear.

There is no fear in love; but perfect love casts out fear, because fear involves torment. But he who fears has not been made perfect in love (1 John 4:18).

If you fear anything, you do not understand or have confidence in the love God has for you. God loves you more than any earthly parent could. He is love, and His ability to care for you goes far beyond human ability. Knowing this, you have no reason to fear. His care is as consistent as His unfailing love.

If God cares about your food and clothes, why wouldn't He care about all the other issues you may face? That negative doctor's diagnosis, the overwhelming debt, and the shaky marriage? You can trust Him with it all, but you have your part to play to receive that care: do not fear.

God considers fear to be a worldly act in response to need. The world doesn't believe in God or His desire and ability to provide or protect. On its own, the world strives to meet its own needs. This self-provision ultimately leads to lack because the world was never meant to be self-sustaining apart from God. He is nowhere near its feeble efforts because no faith was put in Him.

> "And do not seek what you should eat or what you should drink, nor have an anxious mind. For all these things the nations of the world seek after, and your Father knows that you need these things" (Luke 12:29-30).

Instead of following the world's example, put aside fear and instead trust in your Provider, Protector, and Healer. God knew that this would be a challenge, so He gave you a second responsibility—to seek.

> But seek the kingdom of God, and all these things shall be added to you. "Do not fear, little flock, for it is your Father's good pleasure to give you the kingdom. Sell what you have and give alms; provide yourselves money bags which do not grow old, a treasure in the heavens that does not fail,

where no thief approaches nor moth destroys. For where your treasure is, there your heart will be also (Luke 12:31-34).

If you're focused on seeking God and His kingdom, you won't have time to fear. Seeking God means you consistently read His Word and get it deep inside your heart. It means you spend time with Him, allowing Him to refresh and strengthen you. It means you put more priority on His will and ways than you do on your own. It means investing your time, money, and attention into eternity, however God leads. Then, because of your pursuit of Him, your heart's attention is shifted from personal need to a cause much bigger than yourself. Your lifestyle changes and your fear-thoughts are replaced by God-thoughts. You soon have more confidence in Him than you do in your need.

If you want to see "all these things" added to you, you must put your heart in the right place. You must seek your Source and not the deliverance you need. Decide to rely on the only One who can truly help you, regardless of what is going on in the world. When you choose to act in faith as a child of God, you'll forget your fears and remember that God considers you to be more valuable than the birds.

REST FEARLESSLY

As the God of peace, you will never find Him anxious, fearful, stressed, or frustrated. He does not stir up violence and strife. He is powerful, yet calm and gentle in nature. And He has given that nature to you.

> "Peace I leave with you; My [own] peace I now give *and* bequeath to you. Not as the world gives do I give to you. Do not let your hearts be troubled, neither let them be afraid. [Stop allowing yourselves to be agitated and disturbed; and do not permit yourselves to be fearful and intimidated and cowardly and unsettled.]" (John 14:27, AMPC).

Once again, Jesus commands you not to be afraid. While the devil offers the package of fear, Jesus offers the package of peace. He wants you to receive it—regardless of what's going on around you. You must first receive the gift of peace by faith, then purposefully act on His Word.

> Be anxious for nothing, but in everything by prayer and supplication, with thanksgiving, let your requests be made known to God; and the peace of God, which surpasses all understanding, will guard your hearts and minds through Christ Jesus (Philippians 4:6).

Like faith, peace is not truly present if it isn't first in the heart. It doesn't come from the outside in; it comes from the inside out. If it is true peace then it won't be determined by the situation and atmosphere around you. If the peace can be shattered by an evil report or a frustrating person, it is artificial peace—a counterfeit posing as the real thing. Counterfeit peace will smile and act like everything is fine on the outside when it's really filled with anxiety on the inside. When it's genuine peace, however, storms can blow and the peace will stay, unmoved.

CHOOSE THE PEACE

Refuse to be anxious

Be anxious for nothing ... (Philippians 4:6a)

Your mind may be full of fearful thoughts from the devil, your body shaking in automatic response to what you see or feel. But you can choose whether to receive them or reject them. They are trespassing, but you alone decide if they can stay. If fearful thoughts are left unchecked, they will eventually lodge in your mind and heart. From there they will control your life. When that happens, it's much harder to dispose of them in the future. They will rule out the truth of God's Word because it's what you've come to believe. But if you refuse to tolerate them for even a moment, the devil loses his chance to torment and control you. Like any temptation to sin, God's solution is to take control of the thoughts and to cast them out:

> For the weapons of our warfare are not carnal but mighty in God for pulling down strongholds, casting down arguments and every high thing that exalts itself against the knowledge of God, bringing every thought into captivity to the obedience of Christ, and being ready to punish all disobedience when your obedience is fulfilled (2 Corinthians 10:4-6).

Once you have rejected and cast down thoughts of fear, replace them with the purity of God's Word—thoughts that line up with Philippians 4:8.

> Finally, brethren, whatever things are true, whatever things are noble, whatever things are just, whatever things are pure, whatever things are lovely, whatever things are of good report, if there is any virtue and if there is anything praiseworthy—meditate on these things (Philippians 4:8).

Pray

> …but in everything by prayer and supplication … let your requests be made known to God … (Philippians 4:6b).

Once the fearful thoughts are replaced, God expects you to make your requests for assistance known to Him through your prayers. The Bible says you do not have because you do not ask Him (James 4:2). Once you've made your requests known, you can have faith, or confidence, that He will take care of you just like He promised (1 John 5:14,15). At that point, the peace of God will fill your heart, as the weight of the responsibility is lifted from your shoulders onto His. Once that peace is in your heart, it can impact your mind effectively.

What if you didn't pray in faith concerning your situation? What if you didn't have enough confidence in God to take care of you that you remained silent? In that case, no peace would flood your heart and your mind. You'd be left with the same fear and anxiety that plagued you. It's a lack of peace that comes from a troubled *heart* filled with fear.

Give thanks

>...with thanksgiving ... (Philippians 4:6a)

When you consistently thank God for answering your prayer, it shows God that you believe that He will do exactly what He said He would do. It also keeps you in an attitude of expectation for the impending manifestation of His promise to take care of your needs. As a result, a peace continues to flood your heart.

REST IN PEACE

Jesus's example

Jesus is our perfect example of everything godly, including peace. You will never see in the Bible examples of Him running around in distress. Why should He be stressed and anxious? He knew His authority over evil, so He had no reason to fear. He had faith in God's ability to protect Him, regardless of how strong His opponent seemed. As a result, He continued doing what He intended to do on the earth. He didn't let a circumstance detour His life and routine. He was on the earth on a mission. A lack of peace—spawned by fear and doubt— couldn't detour Him. *He didn't let it.*

An example of this is His boat trip with His disciples in Mark 4:35-41. Jesus initiated going over to the other side of a body of water. A storm arose, but it in the middle of it all, Jesus slept soundly in the stern until the disciples woke Him up with: "Teacher, do You not care that we are perishing?" (vs. 38) Clearly, they didn't trust His love for them or His power to keep them from drowning.

> Then He arose and rebuked the wind, and said to the sea, "Peace, be still!" And the wind ceased and there was a great calm. But He said to them, "Why are you so fearful? How is it that you have no faith? And they feared exceedingly, and said to one another, "Who can this be, that even the wind and the sea obey Him" (vs. 39-40)!

Imagine what Jesus slept through. The atmosphere

would have been dark, wet, and cold as rain poured from raging thunderclouds. From those thunderclouds came piercing flashes of lightening and roaring thunder. Agitated by the tumultuous waves, the boat tossed about like a beach ball in the ocean—a perfect invitation for nausea. All about the ship the disciples shouted at each other in panic as they defended their lives against the storm. With the ship teetering at different angles, threatening to sink with the water filling it, slimy fish were likely pouring in and flopping about in confusion. And what was Jesus doing amid all the noise? *Sleeping on a pillow.*

It's unlikely most people could be calm through such chaos, yet alone *sleep*. But Jesus did, to the point that the disciples had to wake Him up. When He did wake up, His response was still drastically different than the disciples' distress. He didn't give in to panic and fear. He took control of the situation with fearless strength and commanded the storm to stop with these words: "Peace be still!" Instead of floundering in the middle of the chaos, He passed His inner peace onto the scene. Functioning in that peace, He was able to use the authority He had been given to bring calm. He knew that without faith, there would be no peace. And without faith and peace working together, there would be no confidence in His ability to tell the storm what to do.

The disciples could have done the same, except they had no faith. Their fear hindered them from using their authority—the same authority Jesus gave them to cast out demons. All they could see was the storm instead of the possibility of God's power manifesting to aid them. While they *focused* on the storm, their minds stayed in anxiety, effecting their actions. They were so paralyzed by what they felt and saw that they could only imagine the worst. Their hearts were too full of fear for their minds to be at peace.

Peter's Example

When reading this story, you may think, "But that's Jesus. He's the Son of God. He was perfect and hasn't experienced what I have."

Jesus lived in a body just like yours. He experienced the same temptations to sin as you do. "For we do not have a High Priest who cannot sympathize with our weaknesses, but was in all points tempted as we are, yet without sin" (Hebrews 4:15). Jesus just chose not to give in to the sin of fear, and chose to trust God, His promises, and His God-given authority. The Bible instructs you to imitate Him (Ephesians 5:1).

One of the disciples—human like you and me—that learned to imitate Jesus was Peter. He had also been in the boat during the storm. He had another water experience later when he walked on water, only to begin to sink when his eyes got off Jesus and focused on the water around him. Peter obviously learned from his faithless experiences and chose to be fearless like Jesus. Under Herod's rule, he was imprisoned and had every reason to fear (Acts 12:1-8).

The Herod had just killed another disciple and now

was planning Peter's execution. Typical Roman style, Herod put him into prison with enough guards to scare off an army. Historically, these prisons weren't anything like the clean, well-fed prisons of today. Most cells were dark, especially the inner cells. Unbearable cold, lack of water, cramped quarters, and sickening stench from few toilets likely made sleeping difficult and waking hours miserable. This was not a moment of relaxation from the real world; it was torture.

But despite the gross stench, foreboding darkness, and impending execution the next morning, Peter managed to fall asleep between two soldiers. Here, very few of us could relate. This wasn't just a bad doctor's report. It wasn't a home foreclosure or relationship gone badly. This was certain *death*.

How could Peter relax enough to snooze during the final hours of his life? How could he nap with cold, metal chains holding him in place between armed guards? How could he even think of resting when the whole kingdom of Rome and his own countrymen were against him? He was at peace … inspired by faith.

Peter's peace was founded on three truths. First, Peter did not fear death. He counted death through martyrdom as an honor (Philippians 1:21). Next to standing before Almighty God, it meant nothing to him for his life to be threatened by a mortal human being like Herod. Second, he was strong enough to know God would protect him because his life's mission was not complete. Third, he knew the church was praying for him. How could he lose?

Peter had confidence in God's desire and power to deliver him. The faith in his heart moved to become peace in his mind, allowing him to slumber, even when Herod sought to do the worst. The decision to walk in peace and not fear triggered God's ability to move supernaturally. God saw his faith and commissioned an angel to guide him out of the prison ... with two oblivious guards sitting beside him. That's peace!

Both Jesus and Peter could have lost their peace in the middle of their situations. Though Jesus was God's Son, He walked on the earth with a body just like yours. Peter was completely human with a body containing feelings and emotions. At any time, they could have allowed their minds—unguarded by peace—to give in to stress and fear. They could have let their emotions succumb to what *could* happen. But they *chose* not to, resulting in peace that sailed them to victory.

Letting peace rule in your life is not just about you, however. The attitude you project could determine someone else's peace, especially if they don't know how to walk in it. You can maintain your peacefulness and allow it to be a testimony of God's goodness, just like Jesus and Peter did. Others will see it and desire that peace, just as God's goodness led you to repentance (Romans 2:4). Rather than being a stumbling block and stealing what little peace others may have, you can reflect Jesus, the Author and Finisher of your faith ... and your peace.

FIGHT FEARLESSLY

We've studied two examples of people who rested fearlessly in their trying situation. Now let's look at someone who fought without fear. We know him well—David, a man after God's own heart.

In 1 Samuel 17, Israel fought against the Philistines but were getting nowhere because of their secret weapon Goliath. Verse 11 says they were "greatly afraid." When David comes on scene, however, his response is totally different: "What shall be done for the man who kills this Philistine and takes away the reproach from Israel? For who is this uncircumcised Philistine, that he should defy the armies of the living God?" He was indignant and fearless. Why was everyone so fearful of such an ungodly man?… Is there not a cause?"

With confidence, David explained his credentials to King Saul: he had killed a lion and a bear single-handedly. He was confident he could do it again with God's help. Though King Saul offered his armor, David rejected them and stayed with what he was familiar with—a sling and a stone.

As he neared Goliath, the giant threw insults at him, indignant that they should send a child. This didn't faze David. He moved forward with confidence, prophesying his victory before he could see it:

> "You come to me with a sword, with a spear, and with a javelin. But I come to you in the name of the Lord of hosts, the God of the armies of Israel,

whom you have defied. This day the Lord will deliver you into my hand, and I will strike you and take your head from you. And this day I will give the carcasses of the camp of the Philistines to the birds of the air and the wild beasts of the earth, that all the earth may know that there is a God in Israel. Then all this assembly shall know that the Lord does not save with sword and spear; for the battle *is* the Lord's, and He will give you into our hands" (v. 45-47).

David "hurried and ran" fearlessly toward the army. Just as he said, his stone sunk deep into Goliath's head, killing Goliath. David then drew out Goliath's sword and killed him with Goliath's own weapon. Later, he arrived at the king's tent with Goliath's head in hand. As a result of his conquest, Israel won a great victory over the Philistine army and David won his reward—no tax payment and the hand of the king's daughter in marriage.

Let's look at a few of David's characteristics that enabled him to fight fearless and win:

A LIFESTYLE OF HOLINESS

Note that David didn't have a sudden rush of bravery when he learned of the problem Israel faced. He lived a life of victory *before* he met Goliath. He practiced fearlessness when he killed the lion and bear. But he also lived a life of obedience to his father, was faithful steward with his shepherd assignment, and spent time building his relationship with God through worship. This kept the favor of God upon his life and prepared him for even bigger responsibilities. By following David's example, you can live the life of a victor, no matter how big or small the challenge or responsibility.

If you want to see victory in your life, a lifestyle of godliness is required. It's not just an investment into your relationship with God. It's also an investment into future victories. Like David, how you live on a day-to-day basis will determine how you fight your battles.

FAMILIARITY WITH GOD'S WORD

The Israelite army did not listen to God's Word—a voice that declared their victory if they would trust Him. Because they gave in to fear, this army could only hear the lies of their spiritual enemy, the devil, speaking to them through their physical enemy. David, on the other hand, was familiar with God's Word and trusted it. He trusted it so much that he rejected the king's armor and chose to use a stone and a sling as his familiar, God-ordained weapon.

Like David, your greatest familiarity should be with the Word of God because it never fails or changes. Fear will put up a screen that will shut off any other voice that may bring a message of hope. By putting God's Word as top priority, you won't have to spend precious time digging into its pages for a solution when giants arrive. You are far more down the road to seeing your victory if your weapon is already warmed up, comfortable, and hanging from your hip.

CONFIDENCE IN GOD'S POWER

Goliath was over nine feet tall. His armor was comprised of a bronze helmet, a coat of bronze mail, bronze armor on his legs, and a bronze javelin. The Bible says the staff of his spear was like a weaver's beam (1 Samuel 17:7). He was an intimidating sight. David, however, remembered clearly how God's power had been faithful to him when he was confronted with a lion and bear. He was not intimidated by what he saw.

As a person of faith, look beyond the natural and focus on the supernatural power of God. The key is to consider the armor *you* wear and what God you serve—both much bigger and much stronger than your problems. God does not change (Malachi 3:6). If He moved on your behalf before, He will do it again!

WORDS OF FAITH

David let Goliath know exactly what the outcome of the fight was going to be—death for Goliath and victory for Israel. And he wasn't afraid to tell his opponent. It wasn't out of arrogance, but true confidence that his trust in God was going to pay off.

You can do the same by declaring God's perfect promise over your life, not just out of routine, but out of faith from your heart because you know it's true. If you have confidence in God's Word, you will have confidence to speak it. Faith speaks and expects to see results.

***

Resisting fear may be challenging. The presence of your problem will try to tell you that you won't win. Like Goliath, the devil will try to belittle who you are and recount your demise. Like David's brothers, others may criticize you for your confidence. You may even be tempted to deal with your fear by relying on natural means. But if you stand your ground, unmoving in your faith, you will see your giant topple. And you can expect not only victory, but a great reward!

> A good man deals graciously and lends; He will guide his affairs with discretion. Surely he will never be shaken; the righteous will be in everlasting remembrance. He will not be afraid of evil tidings; His heart is steadfast, trusting in the Lord. His heart is established; He will not be afraid, until he sees his desire upon his enemies (Psalm 112:5-8).

CHAPTER 7

YOU STAND WITH PRAISE AND THANKSGIVING

PRAISE AND THANKSGIVING are two of the most forgotten weapons when fighting the good fight of faith. It's so easy to get caught up in the fight that we forget Who's still on the throne, and Who's the Author of the foundation we stand on. He deserves our praise and thankfulness—regardless of what's going on in our lives, good or bad. He is God and there is no other God besides Him (Isaiah 44:6). He is our loving, good Creator and Savior who has done wonderful things for us—even when hardship looms over our heads (Psalm 103). If He can rejoice over us, as human as we are, we can certainly worship and give Him thanks in *every* season of life (Zephaniah 3:17).

I will bless the LORD at all times; His praise shall continually be in my mouth (Psalm 24:1).

I will call upon the LORD, who is worthy to be praised; so shall I be saved from my enemies (Psalm 18:3).

Not only does He deserve our praise, but He has also *commanded* us to praise: "Let everything that hath breath praise the Lord!" (Psalm 150:6) If we're breathing, it is our responsibility to praise Him. It doesn't say to praise Him when times are good. It doesn't say to praise Him when we feel like it. It simply says to praise Him if we are alive and breathing, not matter who we are!

Then a voice came from the throne, saying, "Praise our God, all you His servants and those who fear Him, both small and great"! (Revelation 19:5)

Yes, your mind and body may not feel like worshiping God in the middle of a trial, but your born-again spirit with His nature inside desires to worship Him (John 4:23). It desires to be in His presence, adoring Him as your Abba Father. It is a natural response born from a love relationship between God and His child.

Like everything God commands you to do, He has promised blessings to follow. These benefits are priceless. You need them in every part of your life. Though they shouldn't be the final reason you worship, you can expect them, knowing God is faithful.

Praise and worship:

- Invites the presence of God (2 Chronicles 5:11-14)
- Brings victory (2 Chronicles 20:15-20)
- Brings deliverance from enemies (Psalm 18:3)
- Satisfies the soul (Psalm 63:1-5)
- Repels depression (Isaiah 61:3)
- Brings liberty (Acts 16:25, 26)
- Brings joy (Psalm 100:4; Psalm 16:11)
- Draws men to God (John 12:32)
- Strengthens your faith (Romans 4:20)
- Brings you closer to God (James 4:8)

These are more than enough reasons to inspire worship! In times crisis, they are like secret weapons that only you can wield … and the devil cannot stop.

THE GARMENT OF PRAISE

In February 2015, twenty-one Christian young men were marched onto a stretch of Libyan beach. They were forced to kneel in the sand while their captors, dressed in black, stood above them with knives in hand. For refusing to deny their faith, they were pushed to the ground and viciously beheaded. It was an unjust persecution that calls for justice; but despite it all, these men are now heroes of the faith. They willingly laid their lives down for their Lord. They are a testimony to us all in more ways than one.

One detail that stands out to me is the way they left this earth. Unlike most people, they did not kneel in the sand begging for mercy. They did not cry out with child-like fear. No words of anger or hate toward their captors came from their mouths. No, it was the beautiful sound of praise to their Savior that left their lips. It was their final sacrifice of worship toward the One for whom they were dying.

You may never be called to give your life for your faith in this way. But you will have many opportunities to give a sacrifice of praise when you don't feel like it (Hebrews 13:15). Especially in a culture of physical pampering and indulgences, a tempting response to hardship is to cry and whine to any listening ear. If you encounter this temptation, however, you must choose to put on a beautiful piece of spiritual clothing instead—the garment of praise.

> "The Spirit of the Lord God is upon Me, because the Lord has anointed Me to preach good tidings to the poor; He has sent Me to heal the brokenhearted, to proclaim liberty to the captives, and the opening of the prison to those who are bound; to proclaim the acceptable year of the Lord, and the day of vengeance of our God; to comfort all who mourn, to console those who mourn in Zion, to give them beauty for ashes, the oil of joy for mourning, the garment of praise for

the spirit of heaviness; that they may be called trees of righteousness, the planting of the LORD, that He may be glorified."

This is Isaiah prophesying of Jesus long before Jesus read it of Himself in the temple during His earthly ministry (Luke 4:17-21). We are most familiar with verse 1 and 2, but the prophecy continues. Jesus didn't just come to forgive our sins, heal our bodies, and provide for our needs. He also came to "heal the brokenhearted." What is one way He does this? By giving us the garment of praise to replace the spirit of heaviness.

Before I met my husband, I experienced deliverance from the spirit of heaviness through worship. I went on date with someone sent by the devil to side-track me from my husband, whom at the time I had not yet met. This man was rebounding and showed evidence of lustful behavior. After a brief time of communication, I ended all association. Though I didn't feel sorry for disappointing him, heaviness hovered over me like an ugly black cloud. For days I couldn't shake it, regardless of whether I was at home or at work. I couldn't explain it, but I didn't know what it was or what to do.

Finally, as I drove home from work one day, a light bulb flickered on in my heart. I know it was the Holy Spirit speaking to me. I was a child of God! I didn't have to walk around depressed and bogged down. Once in my house, I went straight to my CD player, inserted my favorite praise and worship CD, and cranked it up. With all my heart I let my praise reach heaven. As I did, the heaviness lifted, and I never felt it again.

God doesn't force you to put on that garment. He offers it to you, but you must choose to receive it and put it on. Very rarely will you feel like it, especially when your mind is filled with what you're dealing with. But the key is to by-pass your feelings and put it on by faith, confident that you will see positive results!

What does putting on the garment of praise do?

- It shows God that you're trusting Him and giving Him permission to work on your behalf.
- It forces the spirit of heaviness to leave.
- It allows the oil of joy to flow into your life.
- It causes you to grow strong and stable like a deeply rooted tree.
- It glorifies the Tailor who designed your garment.

BIBLE EXAMPLES OF PRAISE

Paul and Silas

Acts 16 tells the powerful story of Paul and Silas putting on that garment in the middle of hardship. They were being jailed for casting out a demon. With painful stripes on their backs, singing would be the last thing someone would expect. They knew the power of their worship, however, and lifted their voices: "But at midnight Paul and Silas were praying and singing hymns to God …" (Acts 16:25)

Notice what time of night it was. Midnight is not the usual hour to sing. Paul and Silas were human, and I'm certain they desired to rest should their painful backs allow. I'm confident they had to fight angry emotions toward their guards and the ones who unjustly beat them. Bravely, however, they sang for all the jail to hear. The result? Everyone in the prison heard of the greatness of God. The jailer and his entire family were saved. God sent an earthquake, and they were set free (vs. 26-34).

What if they had not put under their physical and mental desires? What if they had ignored their spirits' urge to sing in their bondage? What if they had sulked in the corner pouting? The result would not have been miraculous. God does not move in response to mournful self-pity. It was their praise that created their deliverance, and it was their praise that produced their testimony!

King Jehoshaphat

Another example of powerful praise at work is that of the children of Israel under the leadership of King Jehoshaphat (2 Chronicles 20). One horrific day, the king received news that *multiple* pagan countries were coming against them. Fear was the immediate result. Instead of completely giving into that fear, King Jehoshaphat "set himself to seek the Lord" (v. 3). After he and his nation prayed, God sent a prophet to declare the result of this battle should they move forward in faith: "You will not need to fight in this battle. Position yourselves, stand still and see the salvation of the Lord, who is with you, O Judah and Jerusalem!' Do not fear or be dismayed; tomorrow go out against them, for the Lord is with you" (v. 17).

The next step I believe is crucial. They bowed themselves down and worshiped God, with "voices loud and high" (v. 18-19). They didn't wait until they were desperate in the heat of battle to give God glory. They spiritually prepared themselves *beforehand*, believing God was going to do just what He said.

They then assembled the people and instrumentalists together and marched their way into the wilderness. I could imagine that their emotions screamed at them: "Are you crazy? A weapon of worship? You'll be slaughtered!" Despite the doubts, they continued ... and the result was powerful. God had set an ambush against their enemies before they ever arrived at the battle ground. What lay before them was a mass of dead enemies and so much spoil they couldn't carry it all (v. 24-25)!

It's true that God is the one who fights your battles, but there are actions of faith you must take before God can move. One action is that you create an atmosphere of worship. Your victory is won, not by your whine, but by your admittance that God is greater than the problem. That admittance is done through your praise and God's power in it. Psalm 22:3 says, "But You are holy, enthroned in the praises of Israel." God is where your praise is!

Those martyred Egyptian men on the beach went through far more than you will likely have ever have to endure. You may never have to leave a country to find provision for your family. You may never spend weeks in prison being tortured for your faith. You may never feel the hot breath of your captor in your face demanding that you give up your faith in Jesus. And you may never be forced to sacrifice your physical body at the blade of a knife. These twenty-one young men, all with families, did all this ... yet with praise on their lips.

I had a friend who died in a car accident due to inclement winter weather. When the medics arrived, she was still alive. What was so powerful is that she was worshipping Jesus, even though she was dying. Though it's not God's will for you to die in a car accident, Andrea's response to catastrophe and death came from what was inside of her. Worship and praise came pouring out of her heart because a worshipper is who she was—in the good times and the bad.

The question is this: Will you rise to that same level of worship in the middle of your hardship? Will you praise the Lord, even when your body hurts? Will you lift His Name while your bank account sits empty? Will you rejoice in your God when a relationship goes sour? Will you worship when those you love reject you? Every moment of praise is worth it, because when you make His Name glorious, you will see the miraculous!

Once you put that garment of praise on, be sure to wear it daily—regardless of life's weather. When your life is peaceful, it's easy to let your guard down and begin to slip from your garment of praise. Once out of that garment, however, it's harder to put it back on when trouble come your way. On the other hand, when you live a lifestyle of wearing it 24/7 like Andrea, your automatic response will be to praise. It will come naturally because it's who you are and what you do.

> I will love You, O LORD, my strength. The LORD is my rock and my fortress and my deliverer; my God, my strength, in whom I will trust; my shield and the horn of my salvation, my stronghold. I will call upon the LORD, who is worthy to be praised; so shall I be saved from my enemies (Psalm 18:1-8).

THE POWER OF THANKSGIVING

Let's review 1 John 5:14-15: "Now this is the confidence that we have in Him, that if we ask anything according to His will, He hears us. And if we know that He hears us, whatever we ask, we know that we have the petitions that we have asked of Him."

Sometimes the answer to your prayers manifests immediately for you to see or feel. But sometimes it takes time. What will you choose to do while you're waiting for the answer to appear? Question whether you're going to get it? Complain and express frustration that you don't see it? Or show thankfulness for what God has already promised?

Consider this example: A trustworthy person you know announced that they had deposited a thousand dollars into your bank account. Would you rush to the bank to verify that their words were true? Would you consult other people to confirm that the person had really done what they said? Or would you say "Thank you!" and perhaps follow it up with a handshake or hug?

God is no different. He is trustworthy. You know Him well. Why would you doubt that He gave you exactly what you asked Him for? Faith doesn't doubt but follows up the request with heart-felt thankfulness. This thanksgiving before the manifestation is evidence of your faith that you already have what you've been standing for. According to Philippians 4:6, thanksgiving is the appropriate response following prayer: "Be anxious for nothing, but in everything by prayer and supplication, with thanksgiving, let your requests be made known to God …"

In a world comprised of people whose goal is to get what they can the fastest and easiest way possible, thankfulness has become a lost art. We see people demanding benefits even though they already have much at their disposal. You hear news of people discontent with their possessions, health, and relationships, yet who ignore the many people in the world that have so little. The demand for more and the ungratefulness for less has turned the world sour. According to 2 Timothy 3:1-4, the lack of thanksgiving is listed among the sins that mark the End Times before Jesus returns. You may not normally think of it as a sin, but God finds being unthankful as repulsive as disobedience and greed.

Let's look at a classic thankfulness story found in Luke 17:11-19:

> Now it happened as He went to Jerusalem that He passed through the midst of Samaria and Galilee. Then as He entered a certain village, there met Him ten men who were lepers, who stood afar off. And they lifted up their voices and said, "Jesus, Master, have mercy on us!" So when He saw them, He said to them, "Go, show yourselves to the priests." And so it was that as they went, they were cleansed. And one of them, when he saw that he was healed, returned, and with a loud voice glorified God, and fell down on his face at His feet, giving Him thanks. And he was a Samaritan. So Jesus answered and said, "Were there not ten cleansed? But where are the nine? Were there not any found who returned to give glory to God except this foreigner?" And He said to him, "Arise, go your way. Your faith has made you well."

This story is an example of Jesus's willingness and ability to heal the sick. It is also an example of thankfulness. Out of the ten lepers, one man alone came back to express gratitude. En route to share his testimony, this man suddenly realized that another Person deserved honor. That Jesus's miracle-working power went to work for him was more than enough to inspire a grateful heart. From this story, we can learn some important lessons:

REMEMBER THANKSGIVING

Sadly, the other nine lepers were too engrossed in their excitement to pay Jesus a second visit. They forgot to recognize the One who made their healing possible. Unlike the Samaritan, never get so distracted by your blessing that you fail to acknowledge the Source. Distractions may come in the form problems, a craving for more blessings, or the inability to recognize who your Source really is. If you get distracted for a moment, stop and return to your Master to show your appreciation. His blessings await you!

REMEMBER WHO YOU ARE

The grave commentary of the other nine lepers is that they left the praise and thanksgiving to a foreigner. The thankful leper was a Samaritan who didn't have any right to the covenant blessings the Jews enjoyed. Instead of rushing away, the Israelite countrymen should have set the example by acting out of their honored role as Jews. Just as they did, you may be tempted to leave your role as thankful Christians to someone else. You may find yourself slipping out of your honorable position as a king and priest by forgetting your heritage. But as a Jesus-follower, never let your trademark of gratefulness disappear. The Kingdom of God relies on your royal representation!

FORGET THE CROWD

The Samaritan could have followed his leper friends' example and rushed off to see the priest with no thought to the Man left behind. He could have been more concerned about his reputation and following protocol than for what thankfulness would demand. Instead, he abandoned the thought of "fitting in" and hurried back to the Master. As the world wears on you, you too may be tempted to "conform" to the world (Romans 12:2). You may be feeling pressured to complain like the rest of an ungrateful culture in the Last Days. But if you are a thankful disciple, your heart will be more toward loving Him with thanksgiving than in feeling comfortable with your peers. The result will be honor from the One to Whom You are thankful!

MAKE THANKSGIVING LOUD

Notice the Samaritan's thanksgiving was not done casually! With a loud voice he came hurrying back to Jesus. He didn't just stand before Jesus and shake his hand; he fell at His feet as a sign of worship. He didn't care who saw his show of thanksgiving because he understood that true thankfulness doesn't care who is listening. It expresses itself loudly!

Will you always *feel* like giving thanks for God's goodness in your life, especially before you see the answer to your prayers? No. That's why God gives this command:

> ... in everything give thanks for this is the will of God in Christ Jesus for you (1 Thessalonians 5:18).

Notice that it says "*in* everything give thanks." God hasn't asked you to give thanks *for* everything, but to have a thankful attitude regardless of what's going on around you or to you. Naturally, at times you will *feel* like keeping your focus on what seems wrong. But when you make the choice to put your feelings aside and focus on what God has done for you, your feelings will change. Your heart will begin to overflow with gratefulness as you remember. As you vocalize your thanksgiving, suddenly what seems wrong will pale in comparison to the blessings that you've forgotten—and the blessing you're expecting. And you know they will come for your natural eyes to see because He's a God who keeps His Word!

The most important result of thanksgiving is that it brings glory to God. While complaining keeps your focus on yourself and what seems wrong, thanksgiving turns your attention toward God and His goodness. People around you will hear your testimony and will see God for who He really is. It begins a cycle of recognizing the nature of God and His power. The more people hear your thanksgiving and praise, the more people will put their trust in the Lord and have reason to be thankful as well (Psalm 40:3)!

> Oh, give thanks to the LORD, for He is good! For His mercy endures forever (Psalm 107:1).

CHAPTER 8

YOU STAND IN LOVE AND FORGIVENESS

"WHAT DOES LOVE have to do with standing strong in my battle?" you might ask. It has everything to do with it. In fact, you can know your redemption and believe God's Word, but without love, your faith—and all your other weaponry—will be useless. Faith's ability to work is based on love. When you understand the love God has for you, you can have confidence in His faithfulness to answer your prayer and see you through tough times. And when you act on that love by showing it toward others, you keep your conscience clear and covenant God intact. This maintains your faith so you can receive answers to your prayers.

> For in Christ Jesus neither circumcision nor uncircumcision avails anything, but faith working through love (Galatians 5:6).

God is love (1 John 4:8). As the Author of faith and the One who gives you faith (Romans 12:3), you can exercise your faith through Him. As a just God, He does not ask you to operate out of something you do not have. Just like He has given you a measure of faith to begin your walk with Him, He has given you love. It's not just His love *toward* you, but His love *in* you so you can operate in it.

> Now hope does not disappoint, because the love of God has been poured out in our hearts by the Holy Spirit who was given to us (Romans 5:5).
>
> But the fruit of the Spirit is love ... (Galatians 5:22)

If you have received Jesus as your Lord and Savior, you can operate in faith because of the love of God working in you. The new birth you experienced when you were born again was the result of God's love through sending Jesus to die on the cross. Out of that new birth comes a nature that you cannot have unless you have Love on the inside of you. It's great to have the love of God in you, but God has called you to take it a step further. You are called to be like Him, imitating His love nature in your life (Ephesians 5:1).

THE LOVE OF GOD

What exactly does God's love look like—toward you and toward others through you? The world gives all kinds of ideas on what love looks like and what it should be. But without knowing God and His Word, it is impossible to know what love is.

> For this reason I bow my knees to the Father of our Lord Jesus Christ, from whom the whole family in heaven and earth is named, that He would grant you, according to the riches of His glory, to be strengthened with might through His Spirit in the inner man, that Christ may dwell in your hearts through faith; that you, being rooted and grounded in love, may be able to comprehend with all the saints what is the width and length and depth and height— to know the love of Christ which passes knowledge; that you may be filled with all the fullness of God (Ephesians 3:14-19).

God's greatest desire is that you be "rooted and grounded" in the love of God. This can only occur when Jesus is dwelling in your heart through your faith in Him—something the world knows nothing about.

Let's look at two kinds of love, human love and God's love:

Philadelphia (fil-ad-el-fee-ah)
The US city of Philadelphia, nicknamed The City of Brotherly Love, is named after this word. Brotherly love is the Greek meaning of the word and is the kind of affection you have for friends. The Bible speaks of it in Romans 12:10 as showing the same love for a friend as you would a family member.

Storge (stor-gay)
This form of love is talking about the natural affection you have for your family. This word is not found in the Bible, but its opposite, *astorgos*, is spoken of in Romans 1:31 to describe a loveless generation without natural affection for family members.

Eros (her-ohs)
Though this word, too, cannot be found in the Bible, it means the sexual attraction men and women have for each other. This was designed by God as well, but it gets confused by the world as being love when they enjoy sex before they're married. According to God's Word, it can be an expression of love after marriage; but is an expression of lust before marriage.

Agape (a-gop-e)
This is the highest form of love and comes from the heart of God. It is perfect and pure and is found many places in the Bible, including in the verse that tells us "God is love" (1 John 4:8).

God's *agape* love goes far beyond where human love could ever go. It's not based on simple affection, likes or dislikes, or even feelings. While human, physical love thrives on a daily diet of ever-changing emotion, *agape* love is constant and has nothing to do with the feeling of the moment.

To be true God-love, feelings and temperaments should never be the deciding factor. Jesus knew this well. He didn't feel like showing the greatest act of love we would ever know. We see that from the great drops of blood He sweat in agony in the garden (Luke 22:44). Based on His second prayer, it was plain that it took all the will power and grace of God to go through with it. But because His perfect nature of love, He chose to overcome His feelings and lay His life down. This is true love.

> He went a little farther and fell on His face, and prayed, saying, "O My Father, if it is possible, let this cup pass from Me; nevertheless, not as I will, but as You will"... Again, a second time, He went away and prayed, saying, "O My Father, if this cup cannot pass away from Me unless I drink it, Your will be done" (Matthew 26:39, 42).

Jesus had to make multiple decisions to overcome His human desires and act on *agape* kind of love. He didn't allow fickleness to drive Him away from God the Father's plan. Can you imagine where we'd be today had He given into His feelings? We'd be forever separated from God, on our way to an eternity in Hell. Jesus saw what the outcome of His decision would be and stayed focused. He didn't focus on His tormenting emotions, but on the love He had for His Father and the love He had for us. This is *agape*.

Your mind and body won't always *feel* love for Jesus and love for others. You may not even feel like a Christian because of stress or lack of sleep. That's why your love for Him and others should come from a deep dedicated *agape* love that exceeds *phileo*, *storge*, or *eros*.

1 Corinthians 13 describes *agape* in detail. It begins with another strong truth that's easy to forget in the Christian world. Just like your love isn't determined by feelings, it cannot be determined by good works.

> If I [can] speak in the tongues of men and [even] of angels, but have not love (that reasoning, intentional, spiritual devotion such as is inspired by God's love for and in you), I am only a noisy gong or a clanging cymbal. And if I have prophetic powers (the gift of interpreting the divine will and purpose), and understand all the secret truths *and* mysteries and possess all knowledge, and if I have [sufficient] faith so that I can remove mountains, but have not love (God's love in me) I am nothing (a useless nobody). Even if I dole out all that I have [to the poor in providing] food, and if I surrender my body to be burned *or in order that I may glory*, but have not love (God's love in me), I gain nothing. (I Corinthians 13:1-3, AMPC).

You could operate in the spiritual gifts, have faith that moves mountains, sacrifice your earthly goods, and give up your life to martyrdom, but it it's not done in love, it means nothing. God is first and foremost looking at the state of your heart before he looks at your actions. Again, like Galatians 5:6 says, true faith and its corresponding actions can only be legitimate if it's done through love.

What are the corresponding actions to the *agape* love of God? They are found in verses I Corinthians 13:4-13. We will read it in the New King James Version:

> Love suffers long and is kind; love does not envy; love does not parade itself, is not puffed up; does not behave rudely, does not seek its own, is not provoked, thinks no evil; does not rejoice in iniquity, but rejoices in the truth; bears all things, believes all things, hopes all things, endures all things. Love never fails. But whether there are prophecies, they will fail; whether there are tongues, they will cease; whether there is knowledge, it will vanish away. For we know in part and we prophesy in part. But when that which is perfect has come, then that which is in part will be done away. When I was a child, I spoke as a child, I understood as a child, I thought as a child; but when I became a man, I put away childish things. For now we see in a mirror, dimly, but then face to face. Now I know in part, but then I shall

know just as I also am known. And now abide faith, hope, love, these three; but the greatest of these is love.

Pure love is selfless. And unlike the spiritual gifts, it will not die. It's even greater than faith. It's greater than hope—your confident expectation in what God will do. Why? Because both are rooted in love and cannot operate without it.

A HINDRANCE TO VICTORY

There are several hindrances to victory and answered prayer. The most common hindrance is a lack of faith or doubting God's Word. Sometimes this can be based on insufficient study of God's Word necessary to build faith to receive. Unrepentant sin also hinders you from receiving from God. He cannot legally honor you if you are going against His will and breaking the covenant you have with Him without repenting (1 John 3:21-22, Psalm 66:18, John 9:31, James 4:3). Trusting in people rather than God can also keep you from overcoming, as well as being complacent and lukewarm in your relationship with God.

Here we'll talk about the faith-hindrance of not walking in love with others. Yet loving others is the second greatest commandment and ties in with the first—loving Jesus (Matthew 22:36-40, John 13:34-35).

> In this the children of God and the children of the devil are manifest: Whoever does not practice righteousness is not of God, nor is he who does not love his brother. For this is the message that you heard from the beginning, that we should love one another ... We know that we have passed from death to life, because we love the brethren. He who does not love his brother abides in death. Whoever hates his brother is a murderer, and you know that no murderer has eternal life abiding in him (1 John 3:10-11, 14-15).

Because being at odds with someone in our culture is so normal, you may not realize just how demonic it is. The devil is the author of the sin of strife. He was kicked out of heaven because he rebelled against God—the first example of discord (Isaiah 14:13-14, Luke 10:18).

> Who is wise and understanding among you? Let him show by good conduct that his works are done in the meekness of wisdom. But if you have bitter envy and self-seeking in your hearts, do not boast and lie against the truth. This wisdom does not descend from above, but is earthly, sensual, demonic. For where envy and self-seeking exist, confusion and every evil thing are there. But the wisdom that is from above is first pure, then peaceable, gentle, willing to yield, full of mercy

and good fruits, without partiality and without hypocrisy. Now the fruit of righteousness is sown in peace by those who make peace (James 3:13-18).

He who says he is in the light, and hates his brother, is in darkness until now. He who loves his brother abides in the light, and there is no cause for stumbling in him. But he who hates his brother is in darkness and walks in darkness, and does not know where he is going, because the darkness has blinded his eyes (1 John 2:9-11).

Hate brings death to many areas of life. It breaks apart relationships and destroys peace and health. It can also affect your work and effectiveness in the Body of Christ. And most of all, it affects your relationship with God and your confidence before Him. Receiving an answer to prayer requires faith, but when you know you've done wrong, you cannot confidently stand before God and ask of Him. It also keeps God from hearing your prayer (1 Peter 3:7).

If I regard iniquity in my heart, the Lord will not hear (Psalm 66:8).

Behold, the LORD's hand is not shortened, that it cannot save; nor His ear heavy, that it cannot hear. But your iniquities have separated you from your God; and your sins have hidden His face from you, so that He will not hear (Isaiah 59:1-2).

A sister to strife and anger is unforgiveness. When

you're fighting with someone, you are not letting go of what they have done to you. Rather than halting the strife with forgiveness, you are keeping the offense alive by retaining bitterness. However, God has instructed you to forgive. It's not a suggestion, but something you *must* do to open the door for victory in your life. You are instructed to imitate Him. Only then can He forgive you.

> Therefore, as the elect of God, holy and beloved, put on tender mercies, kindness, humility, meekness, longsuffering; bearing with one another, and forgiving one another, if anyone has a complaint against another; even as Christ forgave you, so you also must do (Colossians 3:12-13).
>
> Let all bitterness, wrath, anger, clamor, and evil speaking be put away from you, with all malice. And be kind to one another, tenderhearted, forgiving one another, even as God in Christ forgave you (Ephesians 4:31-32).
>
> For if you forgive people their trespasses [their reckless and willful sins, leaving them, letting them go, and giving up resentment], your heavenly Father will also forgive you (Matthew 6:14,15, AMPC).

Like love, forgiveness is a choice not based on feelings. Your mind and body might be screaming for you to hold on to strife and retaliate in your defense. But a heart full of God's *agape* love will cry out to forgive. You must make the decision to listen to your Love-filled heart and forgive, even when feelings don't match your actions.

I once had a boss who was cranky and fickle in his moods. He made going to work challenging because I felt like I was on eggshells every time I was around him. I knew God's will was for me to forgive. I didn't feel like it, but every day on the way to work I said, "I forgive John" (name changed for privacy). I also refused to talk bad about him with the other employees. This went on for months. Though my boss didn't change overnight, I continued to receive promotions and raises. A year before I left the company, he had changed his tune. And when I moved to another town, he thanked me for my diligent work and longevity with the company. I'm convinced that had I not chosen to forgive, raises and promotions would not have come. I would not have left with his favor. God would not have been able to promote me to be on staff at a church. I would have sown seeds of discord into my future that would have grown to choke out God's plan because I was in the territory of unforgiveness and strife.

The devil doesn't want you to walk in victory in your life. He'll send the sins of unforgiveness and strife to interrupt your faith walk because He wants you to be like him, and experience defeat like he did. Thankfully, if you fall for his traps, you can repent. God will wipe your slate clean, allowing you to begin again (1 John 1:9). In the case of walking in love, the key is to continue to stand on God's turf of agape love, and *off* Satan's turf of unforgiveness and strife. You can't take authority over evil when you are standing on his territory. Instead, submit yourself to Love so you can resist the devil's ugly temptations and receive the victory God always intended you to possess (James 4:7). Remember, loving others is part of obeying and loving Jesus (John 13:34). God's love has been shed abroad in your heart, so you have the power to love others by not sinning against them (1 Corinthians 13, Romans 5:5, 1 John 3). It's God's grace to continue the pathway of love toward all!

CHAPTER 9

YOU STAND IN HIS STRENGTH

OUR INSTINCT IS to consider ourselves as self-sustaining, able to handle every situation that comes our way. We think we have all the strength we need alone. Unfortunately, believing this makes us a failure because we were never designed to take care of ourselves. We don't have what it takes to conquer every problem, negative feeling, and frustrating experience. Eventually, no matter how smart or strong we think we are, we will fail because our strength isn't enough. It's impossible to do it alone.

> In conclusion, be strong in the Lord [be empowered through your union with Him]; draw your strength from Him [that strength which His boundless might provides] (Ephesians 6:10, AMPC).

"Not by might nor by power, but by My Spirit," says the Lord of hosts (Zechariah 4:6).

You want to come to the place where you consider God as *your* strength. Your confidence should be founded on knowing that His strength is limitless; nothing is too hard for Him (Jeremiah 32:17). The very core of who He is equals strength and power. Unlike human strength, it's unfailing. It's supernatural, not dependent on any source of earthly stamina or ability.

> I will love You, O Lord, **my strength**. The Lord is my rock and my fortress and my deliverer; my God, my strength, in whom I will trust; my shield and the horn of my salvation, my stronghold (Psalm 18:1-2, bold and italics added).
>
> The Lord is my light and my salvation; whom shall I fear? The Lord is the ***strength*** of my life; of whom shall I be afraid? (Psalm 27:1, bold and italics added)

You need God in *every* area of your life—spiritually, mentally, and physically. He desires that you walk in a lifestyle of depending on His strength—not just for the big trials of life, but also the smaller challenges. Your lifestyle, marked by this dependency, does not only turn to Him when the need arises, but focuses on His ability every day of your life. It's far better to draw on His strength before a challenge arrives than when you are right in the middle of it. Whether it's decision-making, physical ability, or success in the workplace, God desires to flex the strength of His arm on your behalf. When you trust that arm, He causes you to soar, not in fluctuating patterns, but higher and higher, stronger and stronger (Psalm 84:7)!

SURRENDER TO HIS STRENGTH

Experiencing God's strength doesn't come automatically just because you're a child of God. There are specific steps you need to take to activate His power. The first step is to humble yourself. It means admitting that you can't handle your trying situation alone, and that you're powerless without your Creator. Only then can you experience God's hand to lift you up.

> Humble yourselves, therefore, under God's mighty hand, that he may lift you up in due time …
> (1 Peter 5:6-7, NIV).
>
> But He gives more grace. Therefore He says: "God resists the proud, but gives grace to the humble" (James 4:6).

Biblical grace is His divine influence on the heart, His unmerited favor, and His empowerment. You can't succeed without it. Even the Apostle Paul thrived on it. Amid intense persecution, He received God's empowerment to endure. If the Apostle Paul needed God's grace, or strength, how much more do you need it (2 Corinthians 12:7-9)?

Following your admittance of your need for Him, act on your belief and "cast your care" on Him. Casting, or throwing, your problems and concerns upon God is an act of humility and trust. Trust is faith—the only way you can access His grace and strength. If you don't trust God enough to throw your cares from your hands to His, He won't have anything to work with to help you. He, however, will not force you to give your care to Him. You must first *choose* to cast your care.

...Cast all your anxiety on him because he cares for you (1 Peter 5:7, NIV).

WAIT ON HIS STRENGTH

Waiting is not something the human nature likes to do. We want immediate results. But according to Isaiah 40, waiting is required if we're going to experience the strength we desire.

Have you not known? Have you not heard? The everlasting God, the Lord, the Creator of the ends of the earth, does not faint or grow weary; there is no searching of His understanding. He gives power to the faint *and* weary, and to him who has no might He increases strength [causing it to multiply and making it to abound]. Even youths shall faint and be weary, and [selected] young men shall feebly stumble *and* fall exhausted; but those who wait for the Lord [who expect, look for, and hope in Him] shall change *and* renew their strength *and* power; they shall lift their wings *and* mount up [close to God] as eagles [mount up to the sun]; they shall run and not be weary, they shall walk and not faint *or* become tired (Isaiah 40:28-31, AMPC).

"Wait" here means to expect and tarry patiently. It does not mean to rush forward and try to solve a situation alone. It simply means to wait as He works, keeping your faith constant rather than becoming impatient with God's timing or speed. Only then will you see the fullness of His promise to provide every ounce of strength He possesses. The outcome of waiting on Him is an endless supply of strength and energy. The result of trusting His strong nature is a straight path and a peaceful mind (Proverbs 4:5-6). When you sense your strength waning, He renews it. When you feel below your problems, you can soar above them. When you feel tired in the journey, you can keep the pace without fainting along the way.

Rest assured, the devil will do all he can to try to stop your faith in God's strength. He'll send doubt and fear to cloud your confidence. He'll tempt you with impatience and frustration when you don't emotionally feel or see His strength in the natural realm. He'll lie to you, trying to convince you that you can manage the situation alone. This is when you have yet another choice—the choice to resist him and the discouraging lies he shares.

If you are *tempted* to believe what the devil says, how you feel, or what others tell you, then you can be confident that your trust in God's strength is working! What does scare the devil is a believer who is wholly confident in the strength of God that belongs to them. They are very aware that it's *His* might, *His* power, and *His* strength that makes them more than conquerors (Romans 8:37)!

> I can do all things through Christ who strengthens me (Philippians 4:13).

Remember the story I told you earlier about my church's summer camp? God did just what He said He would do because I trusted in His strength and not in my own. It's wonderful to know the nature of God and His ability. But just as great is His promise to use that power on your behalf. Numbers 23:19 and Hebrews 6:18 says it's impossible for Him to lie. When He says He will do something, you can have assurance that He will do just what He said He'd do. When He says He is with you, then He is. When He says He is your God, then He is. When He says He will strengthen, uphold, and help you, then you know that's exactly what He will do!

> He gives strength to the weary and increases the power of the weak (Isaiah 40:29).

CHAPTER 10

YOU STAND WITHOUT GIVING UP

LIFE HOLDS MANY races. Our ultimate race is to make it to heaven, but there are other races to run. It could be a race to receive healing in our bodies, recovery for our marriages, or provision for our homes. It could be as simple as obeying God every time He gives us an instruction. Each challenge or goal must be run with faith in God.

Just like a runner in a marathon, don't forget what it takes to reach your finish line. Set your face forward with determination, so you won't be embarrassed by lagging in last place … or not arriving at all (Isaiah 50:7).

> Do you not know that those who run in a race all run, but one receives the prize? Run in such a way that you may obtain it. And everyone who

competes for the prize is temperate in all things. Now they do it to obtain a perishable crown, but we for an imperishable crown. Therefore I run thus: not with uncertainty. Thus I fight: not as one who beats the air. But I discipline my body and bring it into subjection, lest, when I have preached to others, I myself should become disqualified (1 Corinthians 9:24-27).

RUN YOUR RACE

RUN WITH PATIENCE

Wherefore seeing we also are compassed about with so great a cloud of witnesses, let us lay aside every weight, and the sin which doth so easily beset us, and let us run with patience the race that is set before us, looking unto Jesus the author and finisher of our faith; who for the joy that was set before him endured the cross, despising the shame, and is set down at the right hand of the throne of God (Hebrews 12:1-2, KJV).

Patience is not a strong attribute of our culture. We have been spoiled into expecting things within minutes through the constant catering of internet, cell phones, and drive-through restaurants. Even a potential mate can be met within minutes online. With so much instant gratification at our fingertips, the Fruit of the Spirit called patience has melted into the past like a forgotten piece of worn-out clothing (Galatians 5:22, 23).

Patience is having the ability to remain calm and unannoyed when waiting for a lengthy period. In the Greek, it's defined as cheerful endurance or constancy. If we were to truthfully search our lives for this characteristic, I'm sure we'd all come up short at some point. It's not comfortable or gratifying to our bodies or emotions to remain the same, constant person when our desires and needs don't seem to be met the moment we think they should. Our immediate response to a demand to wait turns into a flustered impatience to get what we want *right now*.

Rest assured, God loves to bless you with the desires of your heart (Psalm 37:4). In fact, 1 John 5:14-15 expresses His promise:

> Now this is the confidence that we have in Him, that if we ask anything according to His will, He hears us. And if we know that He hears us, whatever we ask, we know that we have the petitions that we have asked of Him.

God's promise is much like an order placed online. The "orders" you place in prayer could be any number of things: a new car or home, health or strength, a raise at work, or even a husband or wife. Even simple desires of your heart such as a new gadget or set of clothes could qualify as a blessing (Psalm 37:4). Like we studied before, your needs and desires were legally paid for through the blood of Jesus and are part of your inheritance as a child of God. When you select what you desire from God's Word, your faith activates that inheritance so you can receive them. God is just waiting for you to ask, to place your order (John 16:24).

The moment you place an order, God sends a message to the warehouse to load up your merchandise with your name on it. Remember, though, that what you order in life may not always show up for your eyes to see right away. God may send the answer by fax or email. He may choose to send it overnight by a FedEx jet. Or He may choose to make the delivery by snail mail. This is His choice in timing. Or the devil may try to hinder the delivery by influencing people or attacking your situation directly with demonic forces (Daniel 10:11). Regardless of the speed of delivery, the item is still yours. Don't question its existence or your ownership of it. Believe it and wait for its arrival ... patiently.

> ... that we do not become sluggish, but imitate those who through faith and patience inherit the promises (Hebrews 6:12).
>
> For we have need of endurance [patience], so that after we have done the will of God, we may receive the promise (Hebrews 10:36).

You won't receive anything from God by giving up or becoming sluggish. When you're sluggish, you slow down, get frustrated, and contemplate defeat. As a patient person, however, you remain the same as when you started—calm and constant. You still the urge to get impatient and choose to believe that God's promise to keep His Word is just as true as it was when the petition was made. Your faith, not your time spent waiting, is the basis for your patience.

There's a time and a season for everything ... including when your petition arrives for your eyes to see (Ecclesiastes 3:1). God, perfect in His judgment, will never hurt you by sending the answer when the time isn't right. He may have some people and situations to organize first. He may need you to grow in order be able to receive it. He may require you to exercise your faith for a season before you see the answer with your natural eyes. He may expect you to resist the "wiles" of the devil that stand in the way (Ephesians 6:11). Whatever the case, it's your decision whether you rest while you wait, or pout while you doubt.

God, of course, wants to see you succeed as you wait on Him! He wants to see you receive in the natural what He has promised in the spiritual. He desires that you experience that "joy and peace in believing" that He has provided for you (Romans 15:13). He has a "perfect work" He wants to accomplish in and through you, but the only way you will see it is if you are committed to a lifestyle of patience (James 1:4). It's a lifestyle of staying in constant readiness at the front door, expecting the delivery at any moment. It's a decision to never give up, knowing the delivery truck is just around the corner. Unlike the impatient at heart, you simply refuse to leave your patient post lest when the delivery arrives, you're not home to receive it.

RUN WITH FOCUS

There are plenty of distractions to keep you from running your race until the end. Like a cross-country runner, you need to learn to maneuver the rough terrain. Physical weakness, life's problems, negative emotions, and even other people can try to slow your speed and discourage you. Sin and temptation to fulfill your own desires are just as harmful to your race, yet you are called to overcome them all (Hebrews 12:2b, 1 Corinthians 9:27)!

> Therefore we also, since we are surrounded by so great a cloud of witnesses, let us lay aside every weight, and the sin which so easily ensnares us, and let us run with endurance the race that is set before us, looking unto Jesus, the author and finisher of our faith, who for the joy that was set before Him endured the cross, despising the shame, and has sat down at the right hand of the throne of God (Hebrews 12:1-2).

No matter how strong your trust, you will be faced with challenges that come along to break your focus. Most of the time, the discouraging part is the timing. It's the devil's way of getting your focus off the promise and onto the circumstances around you. If he can get you discouraged, he can stop your faith. If he can stop your faith, he can keep you from receiving the answer to your prayer.

Be like the Apostle Paul who said that "none of these things move me" when he was being persecuted; and like Abraham who didn't "consider his own body" when determining the promise of God concerning his future child. They would simply not be moved off their foundation of God's Word (Acts 20:22-24, Romans 4:19-20).

RUN WITHOUT LOOKING BACK

Runners never win by constantly looking back. If you dwell on your past, compare your life to other people, or focus on the problem, you will never reach your checkpoints, much less your finish line. The devil will keep us in bondage by making your past look better than your future, or by telling you that you don't deserve success because of the things you've done. God, however, wants you to focus on Him and the future so you can win your prize (Philippians 3:13)!

> If any of you lacks wisdom, let him ask of God, who gives to all liberally and without reproach, and it will be given to him. But let him ask in faith, with no doubting, for he who doubts is like a wave of the sea driven and tossed by the wind. For let not that man suppose that he will receive anything from the Lord; he is a double-minded man, unstable in all his ways (James 1:5-8).

> He did not waver at the promise of God through unbelief, but was strengthened in faith, giving glory to God, and being fully convinced that what He had promised He was also able to perform. And therefore "it was accounted to him for righteousness" (Romans 4:20-22).

Like people in the bleachers, the world is watching you. Other believers are depending on your testimony to encourage them to run their own race. They need your testimony and what God has given to you to give them. Unbelievers are watching, too, wondering if this race you're running is worth their commitment. God needs you to represent Him and point the way to the finish line (Hebrews 12:1).

> Therefore, having been justified by faith, we have peace with God through our Lord Jesus Christ, through whom also we have access by faith into this grace in which we stand, and rejoice in hope of the glory of God. And not only *that,* but we also glory in tribulations, knowing that tribulation produces perseverance; and perseverance, character; and character, hope. Now hope does not disappoint, because the love of God has been poured out in our hearts by the Holy Spirit who was given to us (Romans 5:1-5).

RUN WITHOUT DROPPING OUT

You will have many opportunities to grow weary in your race. But don't allow yourself to succumb to weariness and give up. Like a runner, stay strong through plenty of fluids, exercise, and a healthy diet. The strength you need comes through a steady diet of God's Word, prayer, and obedience to God's commands. Only those who don't quit finish the race and receive the prize. The Kingdom of God needs you to stay in the race and finish it with joy!

> And let us not lose heart *and* grow weary *and* faint in acting nobly *and* doing right, for in due time *and* at the appointed season we shall reap, if we do not loosen *and* relax our courage *and* faint (Galatians 6:9, AMPC).

CHAPTER 11

YOU STAND WITH CONFIDENCE

FIRST JOHN 5:14-15 is clear that confidence in God is required to receive from Him. Confidence is firm trust that God will keep His side of the covenant—or binding agreement—you have with Him. You may believe and act on His Word for a season, but you may get discouraged when you don't see situations change right away. You may not see how it could possible work out for your good. The only way to combat that temptation to doubt is by building your confidence in who God is and what He will do. You need confidence that He can be trusted, both in His nature and in His power and Word.

CONFIDENCE IN HIS NATURE

It's difficult to find trustworthy people in our culture. A salesman persuades us to buy their product but fails to point out the small print. A politician claims to support one cause, while once in office, says he opposes it. A potential employee boasts of his work experience in an interview but proves incompetent while on the job. Even close friends let us down by neglecting their promises.

God, on the other hand, is entirely trustworthy. He can be trusted, regardless of political gain or the mood of the moment. Unlike selfish humans, His nature is as consistent as His Word. He can be trusted because of His perfect nature of integrity.

HE'S HONEST

While people may give into the temptation to lie for personal benefit, God is not given to breaking His own Ten Commandments. He's not a liar. In fact, it is impossible for Him to lie.

> God is not a man, that He should lie, nor a son of man, that He should repent … (Numbers 23:19a).

> Paul, a bondservant of God and an apostle of Jesus Christ, according to the faith of God's elect and the acknowledgment of the truth which accords with godliness, in hope of eternal life which God, who cannot lie, promised before time began … (Titus 1:1-2).

HE'S FAITHFUL

To be faithful means to be constant, loyal, steadfast, and reliable. When God makes a promise, He is sure to follow through. Though people may fail to keep their word for many reasons, God will not allow one word He says to go uncompleted.

> Your faithfulness endures to all generations; You established the earth, and it abides (Psalm 119:90).
>
> "So shall My word be that goes forth from My mouth; it shall not return to Me void, but it shall accomplish what I please, and it shall prosper in the thing for which I sent it" (Isaiah 55:11).

HE'S LIMITLESS

People have limitations. Their muscles can only get so strong. Their minds can only understand so much. Eventually people will die, leaving behind only a sample of their strength. God's power, however, is limitless and endures forever. Nothing is too hard for Him.

> But Jesus looked at them and said to them, "With men this is impossible, but with God all things are possible" (Matthew 19:26).
>
> Ah, Lord God! Behold, You have made the heavens and the earth by Your great power and outstretched arm. There is nothing too hard for You (Jeremiah 32:17).

HE IS LOVE

God is love. Those who lie and prove undependable are acting out of selfishness, the opposite of love. But God, who is love, operates through that love in everything that He does. First Corinthians 13 is His nature in action, and He proved it with the ultimate example of sacrifice.

> He who does not love does not know God, for God is love (I John 4:8).
>
> He who did not spare His own Son, but delivered Him up for us all, how shall He not with Him also freely give us all things (Romans 8:32)?

HE IS A PERFECT FATHER

Though the world is full of imperfect fathers, God is the perfect example of fatherhood. He does no harm to His children but always seeks their well-being. Many may forsake you, including your parents, but your heavenly Father will never leave you. In their absence, He will take care of you (Psalm 27:10, Hebrews 13:5).

> Ask, and it will be given to you; seek, and you will find; knock, and it will be opened to you. For everyone who asks receives, and he who seeks finds, and to him who knocks it will be opened. Or what man is there among you who, if his son asks for bread, will give him a stone? Or if he asks for a fish, will he give him a serpent? If you then,

being evil, know how to give good gifts to your children, how much more will your Father who is in heaven give good things to those who ask Him (Matthew 7:7-11)!

You will come across many frustrating people and contrary circumstances in your life. People may do you physical harm or slander your good name. They may plot against you, or at the very least, go back on their word. You may face sickness in your body or a shortage in your bank account. You may struggle with depression, fear, or anxiety. You may find yourself bound by addictions and bad habits. In times like these, you need someone reliable to assist you.

People boast of many ways—some good and some bad—that can help you. Counseling sessions, loans, medication, and relationships all hold promise of assistance. Some will provide what you need, but some will disappoint you because it was so short-lived. Some may even lead to your demise because of its imperfection.

When you keep your eyes on fallible people and their methods, you can easily get frustrated and disillusioned.

That's why you need someone who can be trusted, someone who proves constant and dependable. As you see in the verses above, only *one* Person can boast of being 100 percent trustworthy. The God of the universe holds every characteristic worth trusting!

Lean on, trust in, and be confident in the Lord with all your heart and mind and do not rely on your own insight or understanding. In all your ways know, recognize, and acknowledge Him, and He will direct and make straight and plain your paths (Proverbs 3:5-6).

CONFIDENCE IN HIS WORD

Like I listed above, God is a perfect example of faithfulness. Many well-meaning people may attempt to exemplify faithfulness, but they can't hold a candle to God's perfect, promise-keeping nature. His very name is Faithful and True (Revelation 19:11), and He keeps His Word to a "thousand generations" (Psalm 105:8). In fact, Numbers 23:19 says, "God is not a man, that he should lie; neither the son of man, that he should repent: hath he said, and shall he not do it? or hath he spoken, and shall he not make it good?" Hebrews 6:18 confirms that it's *impossible* for Him to lie! With this kind of reputation, there should be no difficulty trusting Him.

Unfortunately, human nature has a challenging time putting full confidence in something—or Someone—we cannot see. We are so led by our five senses that anything out of our physical reach or vision seems impossible. We have been so scarred by examples of unfaithfulness in our lives that we don't want to trust anyone ever again. Even God is added to the list of "do not trust," and we walk away, disillusioned and hardened.

A lack of trust in God's faithfulness is not a new flaw. It started in the Garden of Eden when Eve believed a lie from the devil rather than the truth of God's Word. The distrust continued right up to Jesus's Resurrection, the most glorious day to those who believe in Jesus!

God expects you to believe His Word, so He faithfully gives you a word to believe. He communicated with His disciples the same way, giving them a prophecy of His betrayal, crucifixion, and His resurrection.

> "Behold, we go up to Jerusalem; and the Son of man shall be betrayed unto the chief priests and unto the scribes, and they shall condemn him to death, and shall deliver him to the Gentiles to mock, and to scourge, and to crucify him: and the third day he shall rise again" (Matthew 20:18-19).

These were attention-grabbing words! To those who followed Him for three years, it meant a disbanding of their group and the loss of Someone they had come to love. Regardless of Who said these words, however, the disciples rejected them. They continued as usual, marching joyfully through Jesus's triumphant entry into Jerusalem, oblivious to what lay ahead of them. From then on, every tragic—yet God-ordained—event took them by surprise. Sadly, the doubt in God's faithfulness continued right up to the tomb.

Now after the Sabbath, as the first day of the week began to dawn, Mary Magdalene and the other Mary came to see the tomb. And behold, there was a great earthquake; for an angel of the Lord descended from heaven, and came and rolled back the stone from the door, and sat on it. His countenance was like lightning and his clothing as white as snow. And the guards shook for fear of him, and became like dead men. But the angel answered and said to the women, "Do not be afraid, for I know that you seek Jesus who was crucified. He is not here; for He is risen, as He said. Come, see the place where the Lord lay" (Matthew 28:1-6).

Mary Magdalene and the other Mary left behind their mourning friends and prepared to do what any grieving mourners would do—apply spices to Jesus's body (Mark 16:1). They were prepared, not for a resurrection, but for a corpse, wrapped in burial clothes. They expected guards on site, and a stone inhibiting their entrance. Instead, they found an open tomb and an angel sitting calmly, waiting for their arrival. Within minutes their unbelief in Jesus's third-day resurrection melted into faith and they quickly left to obey the angel's orders.

When the two women left to share the good news of Jesus's resurrection, they were met with further unbelief (Luke 2:11 Mark 16:11, 13). The disciples doubted their words, even though Jesus's previous words backed them up. Later, Jesus was gracious enough to give the unbelieving disciples a refresher course concerning everything He had said before about His redemptive acts (Luke 24:44-49). The talks didn't come without a verbal correction, however. He rebuked them for their hardness of heart and unbelief, the root of their fear and lack of expectation (Mark 16:14). Sadly, even after this, doubt didn't completely leave the clan of disciples.

Even as Jesus stood on the mountain and gave them the great commission, some still doubted (Matthew 28:17).

Unlike God, human nature would have stomped away in disgust after hearing so much unbelief. It would have given up and left all prophecies in the dust because it was too difficult to get support. God, however, cannot lie or change His mind. He has no Plan B. The abortion of a plan is not an option. It might take years of patience as He waits for people to take Him off the "do not trust list." It may take consistent prodding of His presence and repetition of His Word to soften a person's hardened heart. Regardless of what it takes, He knows He will find, in time, someone who will believe His Word and act on it.

God's desire for you is that you be of the believing group and not of the unbelieving. He wants you to believe His Word the first time, followed by expectation that He will do just as He said. He wants you to have confidence in His faithfulness. He wants your faith in Him to go beyond what you can see, reaching for the humanly impossible Resurrection power. To those who believe that power, all things are possible (Mark 9:23)!

Blessed are those who have not seen and yet have believed (John 20:29b).

CONFIDENCE IN HIS POWER

God made us with a unique set of five senses: smelling, tasting, feeling, hearing, and seeing. They are what makes us compatible to live in this natural world He made. Without them, we would self-destruct because we couldn't make solid decisions. We'd burn ourselves if we couldn't sense something was hot. We'd run into things if we couldn't see where we were going. We'd get run over if we couldn't hear the cars coming. We couldn't communicate to save our lives without the use of our mouths. God knew what He was doing when He graced us with these abilities. But even *with* these needed senses, we can still stumble if we choose to live by them *alone*. Neglecting the supernatural, our survival and success in life is limited, and perhaps even fatal. Supernatural is something that is unable to be explained by science or the laws of nature. How many of us operate in the supernatural daily? How many of us expect to see a supernatural miracle in a world dominated by the five senses?

God is a supernatural God and deals supernaturally. As a Christian, you have already experienced His supernatural power. The first supernatural event that happened was when God spoke, and the world came into existence (Genesis 1, 2). You're here because of the supernatural power of God!

The second supernatural even occurred in your life was when you received Jesus as Lord and Savior. God took out the sinful spirit on the inside of you and replaced it with His spirit, sin-free and as perfect as He is. No natural event could have made either of these things happen!

You serve a supernatural God that is unlimited by the natural world you live in. He is a spirit being, supernatural alone in the sense that you can't see Him. But He is also supernatural in the way He operates. Consider some of the greatest Bible stories you may have grown up hearing. If you're like me, you may have heard them so many times that you take them for granted. But they are far from insignificant. In a world that celebrates Superman and the *Twilight* series, these true-life stories from the Bible have been ignored and neglected.

- The Creation of the earth
- The Flood that destroyed the world
- Sarah's pregnancy at an old age
- Israel's deliverance from Egypt
- The Fall of Jericho's walls
- The sun standing still for Israel's victory
- The shutting of lion's mouths to protect Daniel
- Jonah's giant fish rescue
- Mary's pregnancy though she was a virgin
- Hundreds of healing, deliverance, and provision miracles performed by Jesus and the Apostles

The common denominator to all these stories is that they were done for and through people who served and trusted in a supernatural God. They didn't naturally occur simply because someone wished them to or exercised their own power in God's absence. They had supernatural power working on their behalf.

God doesn't operate by human limitations. His mind doesn't even consider the natural when He moves to do something. When a person says something is impossible, God declares that *all* things are possible.

> But Jesus looked at them and said to them, "With men this is impossible, but with God all things are possible" (Matthew 19:26).

You hinder God's ability to operate supernaturally in your life when you forget His supernatural power. When you see catastrophe happening all around you and shake in fear, you stop His supernatural ability to protect you (Psalm 78:41, 42). When you get a bad doctor's diagnosis that's rendered incurable and stay in fear about it, you limit His power to heal you. When you look at your stack of bills and determine that you're going under, you stop His provision from reaching you. Experiencing God's supernatural hand at work in your life is wholly dependent on your *faith* (Matthew 13:58).

Consider Thomas' response to hearing the news of Jesus's Resurrection:

> Now Thomas, called the Twin, one of the twelve, was not with them when Jesus came. The other disciples therefore said to him, "We have seen the

Lord." So he said to them, "Unless I see in His hands the print of the nails, and put my finger into the print of the nails, and put my hand into His side, I will not believe." And after eight days His disciples were again inside, and Thomas with them. Jesus came, the doors being shut, and stood in the midst, and said, "Peace to you!" Then He said to Thomas, "Reach your finger here, and look at My hands; and reach your hand here, and put it into My side. Do not be unbelieving, but believing." And Thomas answered and said to Him, "My Lord and my God!" Jesus said to him, "Thomas, because you have seen Me, you have believed. Blessed are those who have not seen and yet have believed" (Matthew 20:24-29).

If you wait until you see a confirmation in the natural before you believe, your faith is not in a supernatural God. You are insulting God by saying that He is not powerful enough to meet your need without physical means. You are not operating in faith—the faith that says, "Though I haven't seen, I believe."

On the other hand, if you choose to ignore the natural and consider only the supernatural, it opens the door for supernatural intervention from God Himself! Your faith in God alone pleases God to the point that He will make *all* things possible! The biggest problem in your life doesn't stand a chance when confronted by the supernatural power of God. It's not a matter of *how* He will do it that matters; it's knowing and trusting that He *will*—however He chooses!

All through the Bible there are examples of God using unimaginable means to get His job done. Who would have thought a world could be made by just speaking a word? Who would have used trumpets and shouts to fell a wall? Who would have instructed Naaman to dip in the river to be cleansed of his leprosy? What was He thinking? The answer is simple: God was thinking outside the box of human limited ideas and power. He was not constrained by human ideas.

As the Son of God, Jesus's methods didn't go over very well with the religious leaders of the day. He was consistently nudging their boxes off the shelves by challenging them with "he who is without sin among you, let him throw the first stone" (John 8:7). He dented their boxes by eating with unwashed hands (Matthew 15:2). He nearly crushed their boxes when He ate with sinners and forgave sins while healing diseases (Mark 2:13-17; Mark 2:1-12). When He proclaimed Himself as the Son of God and died on the cross, it was all they could do to hold their ideals intact.

God has many methods of solving your problems. He may choose natural means or supernatural means, but regardless, it will be Him. It's not your job to understand; it's your job to obey whatever instructions He gives you. Your job is to keep believing and be at peace knowing He will get it done—by whatever means He sees fit to use.

"'For my thoughts are not your thoughts, neither are your ways my ways,' saith the LORD. 'For as the heavens are higher than the earth, so are my ways higher than your ways, and my thoughts than your thoughts'" (Isaiah 55:8-9).

If God consulted other people's meager ideas for advice on how to run the world, the world wouldn't know God's miracle-working power. Their limited thinking would have tied His hands from performing miracles throughout history. If He followed their legalistic, natural opinions to decide if something would work, many characters in the Bible would never have come out of obscurity. Many great feats would not have been accomplished, and many blessings would not have been made available. Thankfully, God chose to stick to His own "thoughts" and stepped out to do His will, regardless of what anyone else thought.

> But as it is written: "Eye has not seen, nor ear heard, nor have entered into the heart of man the things which God has prepared for those who love Him." But God has revealed *them* to us through His Spirit. For the Spirit searches all things, yes, the deep things of God. For what man knows the things of a man except the spirit of the man which is in him? Even so no one knows the things of God except the Spirit of God. Now we have received, not the spirit of the world, but the Spirit who is from God, that we might know the things that

have been freely given to us by God … For "who has known the mind of the Lord that he may instruct Him?" But we have the mind of Christ (I Corinthians 2:9-12, 16).

Knowing this, you can relax and stop spending your energy making things happen the way *you* think they should. Instead, you can surrender to God's plan, choosing to admit that His ways are higher and smarter than yours. It may be uncomfortable to your physical desires at first. It may cause your insecurities to surface, and your fears to take wing. It will require true *humility* to lay your plans at His feet in surrender. It will require *faith* to think outside your box and into His. But as you do, God will reveal His perfect plan through His faithful Spirit.

CONFIDENCE IN THE FINISHED WORK

Though people may fail to complete what He starts, God always completes His tasks. He does not get discouraged, intimidated, or lazy concerning His projects. He begins … and He finishes.

Many times, however, you may think God has forgotten you and left a project in your life unfinished. When you look at your empty checkbook or aching body, you assume that it's the final product. Your senses take over as you're moved by what you feel and see in the natural. Discouragement sets in and you come to believe that you'll never see God's project finished. At times like these, God's Word is quick to remind you of His consistent nature:

> ... And I am convinced *and* sure of this very thing, that He Who began a good work in you will continue until the day of Jesus Christ [right up to the time of His return], developing [that good work] *and* perfecting *and* bringing it to full completion in you (Philippians 1:6 AMPC).
>
> The LORD will perfect that which concerns me; your mercy, LORD, endures forever; do not forsake the works of Your hands (Psalm 138:8).

To truly receive the best, you must have confidence that He will not only *complete* the work, but also make it a *perfect* work. Looking at Genesis once more, you'll find that God stepped back from His work several times and declared that it was "good." You can trust that His signature of excellence will mark the work in your life as well. It will be perfect! In fact, expect it to exceed your meager imagination!

If God can orchestrate and finish something as complex and significant as the Cross, then He can certainly complete the work He begins in your life. There is nothing too hard for Him (Jeremiah 32:27). From beginning to end, no detail will go untouched if you keep your confidence in the One who finishes His work!

For God is not unjust to forget your work and labor of love which you have shown toward His name, in that you have ministered to the saints, and do minister. And we desire that each one of you show the same diligence to the full assurance of hope until the end, that you do not become sluggish, but imitate those who through faith and patience inherit the promises (Hebrews 6:10-11).

CONCLUSION

THE WOUNDED SOLDIER collapses beneath the weight of his backpack and empty machine gun. Overcome by exhaustion and anxiety, he curls up into a defeated ball. He has no more fight left in him. Defeat seems the only option since his platoon is nowhere to be found and his strength seems to have vanished. All he wants to do is end the fight by surrendering to his enemy. But in his discouragement and despair, he hears his commander's voice ringing in his mind, "Never quit, soldier! Stand to your feet, load your gun, and face your enemy! Victory is just ahead!"

Though strong and authoritative, that voice brings comfort and strength. There was hope. He only needed to press on and use the resources given to him. Gathering as much strength as he could, the soldier reaches into his gear and drinks deeply from his canteen. Then, with trembling hands, he reloads his machine gun. He wouldn't quit. He would fight like the soldier he was trained to be—with confidence and authority. With a surge of strength, he lifts himself from the ground and charges once again through the brush. Enemies face him, but he plows on with his weapon in full use. Suddenly, he stumbles to a stop. Shielding his eyes from the sun's glare, he realizes that he's no longer in the thicket. He is at the top of the mountain, surrounded by his platoon. A cheer goes up from the group of warriors at the sight of him. He had fought ... and he had won.

This story does not have to be simply an inspirational story. It can be *your* victory reality! To see your battles won, I want to encourage you to put the victory guidelines found in this book into practice. Trust God and believe in His unfailing Word. Refuse to give up but depend wholly in God's strength. When you do, without a doubt, you will experience God's love and grace along your faith journey. You will reach your mountaintop victoriously—and come out stronger in the end!

But don't let your story end there. Pass on your victory by sharing the principles you've learned with others. Many around you are suffering and need to know God's victory strategies as well. They need to hear your testimony—and the truth of God's power and faithfulness!

> So let us seize *and* hold fast *and* retain without wavering the hope we cherish *and* confess *and* our acknowledgement of it, for He Who promised is reliable (sure) *and* faithful to His word (Hebrews 10:23, AMPC).

Now to Him who is able to do exceedingly abundantly above all that we ask or think, according to the power that works in us, to Him be glory in the church by Christ Jesus to all generations, forever and ever. Amen (Ephesians 3:20-21).

PRAYER FOR SALVATION

PERHAPS AS YOU'VE read through this book, you've realized that you don't have relationship with God. You haven't experienced His forgiveness and redemptive power in your life, so you don't have the confidence to stand in life's battles. If you desire to experience Jesus Christ's unfailing love for you, God the Father's arms are open wide for you to enter. Joining His family is as simple as rejecting sin and making Jesus the Lord of your life—at no charge to yourself. It is a gift (Ephesians 2:8).

Romans 10:9, 10 says, "That if you confess with your mouth the Lord Jesus and believe in your heart that God has raised Him from the dead, you will be saved. For with the heart one believes unto righteousness, and with the mouth confession is made unto salvation."

If you want God's gift of eternal life, pray this prayer out loud:

> Lord Jesus, I am a sinner in need of a Savior. Because of my sin, I know that when I die I will go to hell. I want to be saved. I turn away from

my sins and I call on the Name of Jesus to save me. Jesus, be my Lord and Savior. Forgive my sins. Give me a new heart and the gift of eternal life. I confess that Jesus is Lord, and I believe in my heart that God raised Him from the dead. Thank you, Jesus, for loving me and saving me. I choose to live for you the rest of my life!

If you prayed this prayer and meant it with all your heart, you are God's child—no longer shackled by the devil and sin. You're now part of God's family and will spend eternity in heaven with Him. As you learn to follow Him, you can experience His goodness in your life. His power will enable you to live in victory over every situation!

APPENDIX A

MY CONFESSION OF FAITH

Compiled by Pastor James Loper

WHO GOD IS TO ME NOW THAT I AM IN CHRIST:

1. He is the Lord My Righteousness (Jeremiah 23:5-6).
2. He is the Lord Who Sanctifies Me (Leviticus 20:8).
3. He is the Lord My Peace (Judges 6:23-24).
4. He is the Lord Who Is Present with me (Ezekiel 48:35).
5. He is the Lord Who Will Provide (Genesis 22:14).
6. He is the Lord Who Heals me (Exodus 15:26).
7. He is the Lord My Banner, my victory (Exodus 17:15).
8. He is the Lord My Shepherd (Psalm 23:1).

9. God is with me (Isaiah 41:10).
10. God is in me (2 Corinthians 6:16).
11. God is upon me (Acts 1:8).
12. God is for me (Romans 8:31).

WHO I AM IN CHRIST:

1. I am saved (Romans 10:8-13).
2. I am born of God (John 1:10-13).
3. I am a new Creation (2 Corinthians 5:17)
4. I am redeemed (Galatians 3:13-14).
5. I am delivered (Colossians 1:12-14).
6. I am justified (Romans 5:1).
7. I am reconciled to God (2 Corinthians 5:18-21).
8. I am sanctified (Hebrews 10:10-14).
9. I am righteous (2 Corinthians 5:21).
10. I am blessed (Ephesians 1:3).
11. I am an overcomer (I John 5:4-5).
12. I am an heir of God (Romans 8:16-17).
13. I am a citizen of heaven (Philippians 3:20).
14. I am free from the power of sin (Romans 6:6-7).
15. I am a member of Christ's body, the church (Ephesians 5:30).
16. I am adopted into God's family (Ephesians 1:5).
17. I am accepted by God (Ephesians 1:6).
18. I am the temple of God and indwelt by the Holy Spirit (2 Corinthians 3:16).
19. I am a friend of God (John 15:13-14).
20. I am a special treasure (I Peter 2:9).

21. I am an ambassador for Christ (2 Corinthians 5:20).
22. I am forgiven (Colossians 2:13-14).
23. I am healed by Jesus's stripes (I Peter 2:24).
24. My old man was crucified with Christ (Romans 6:7).
25. My old man died with Christ (2 Corinthians 5:14).
26. My old man was buried with Christ (Romans 6:3-4).
27. I was raised (Ephesians 2:5-6).
28. I am God's workmanship (Ephesians 2:10).
29. I am holy and unblameable and unreproveable in God's sight (Colossians 1:21-22).
30. I am the friend of Jesus (John 15:13-14).
31. I am called of God (Romans 8:30).
32. I am an able minister of the New Covenant (2 Corinthians 3:6).
33. I am complete in Him who is the head of all principality and power (Colossians 2:10).
34. I am more than a conqueror (Romans 8:37).

WHERE I AM IN CHRIST:

1. I am hidden with Christ in God (Colossians 3:3).
2. I am seated with Christ in heavenly places (Ephesians 2:6).
3. I am abiding in Christ (John 15:1-8).

4. I shall appear with Christ in glory (Colossians 3:4).

WHAT I HAVE IN CHRIST:

1. I have redemption (Ephesians 1:7).
2. I have everlasting life (John 5:24).
3. I have peace with God (Romans 5:1).
4. I have fellowship with the Father and Jesus Christ (1 John 1:3).
5. I have the love of God in my heart (Romans 5:5).
6. I have an inheritance from God (1 Peter 1:3-4, Ephesians 1:11).
7. I have the anointing of the Holy Spirit abiding in me (1 John 2:27).
8. I have the power of the Holy Spirit upon me (Acts 1:8).
9. I have the manifestation of the Holy Spirit (1 Corinthians 12:7).
10. I have authority over the devil and his works (Luke 10:19).
11. I have the right to use the name of Jesus (John 16:23, 24; John 14:12-13).
12. I have everything I ask in prayer according to God's will (1 John 5:14-15).
13. I have access to God's most Holy presence (Ephesians 2:18, Hebrews 10:19).
14. I have the fruit of the Spirit (Galatians 5:22-24).

15. I have the ministry of reconciliation (2 Corinthians 5:18-19).
16. I have deliverance from enemies and freedom from fear (Luke 1:74, 75).
17. I have the victory (1 Corinthians 15:57).
18. I have miraculous ability to witness to the resurrection of Jesus (Acts 1:8).
19. I have the Spirit of power, love, and a sound mind (2 Timothy 1:7).
20. I have the Holy Spirit (2 Corinthians 6:19).
21. I have the mind of Christ (1 Corinthians 2:16).
22. I have the family name (Ephesians 3:14, 15).
23. I have the faith of God (Mark 11:22).
24. I have reconciliation (Romans 5:11).
25. I have access into God's grace (Romans 5:2).
26. I have the right to bring forth fruit and that my fruit would remain (John 15:16).
27. I have the Greater One living in me (1 John 4:4).
28. I have all things that pertain to life and godliness (2 Peter 1:3).
29. I have exceeding great and precious promises (2 Peter 1:4).
30. I have a Great High Priest (Hebrews 10:21).
31. I have a better covenant established upon better promises (Hebrews 8:6).
32. I have whatever I say, if I will not doubt in my heart, but believe that what I say will come to pass (Mark 11:23).

33. I have overcome the spirit of antichrist and the false prophet (1 John 4:4).
34. I have the spirit of faith (2 Corinthians 4:13).
35. I have been predestined unto adoption (Ephesians 1:5).
36. I have the revelation of the mystery of His will (Ephesians 1:9).
37. I have a good conscience (1 Peter 3:16).
38. I have gifts according to the grace given to me (Romans 12:6).
39. I have an abundant life (John 10:10).
40. I have all my needs met according to God's riches in glory by Christ Jesus (Philippians 4:19).
41. I always have all sufficiency in all things and abound to every work (2 Corinthians 9:8).
42. I have an Advocate with the Father (1 John 2:1).
43. I have the Kingdom (Luke 12:32).
44. I have the treasure of God's life and nature in my mortal body (2 Corinthians 4:7).

WHAT I CAN DO IN CHRIST:

1. I can do all things through Christ who strengthens me (Philippians 4:13).
2. I can do the works of Christ (Matthew 9:35, Mark 16:15-18, John 14:12-14, Matthew 4:23-24).
3. I can reign in life (Romans 5:17).

WHAT CHRIST IN ME WILL DO THROUGH ME:

1. I am destined to be glorified by Christ (Colossians 1:27).
2. I am destined to be conformed to the image of Christ (Romans 8:29).
3. The life of Jesus is manifested in my mortal body (2 Corinthians 4:11).

APPENDIX B

CHARACTERISTICS OF THOSE WHO LIVE BY FAITH

WHAT BELIEVERS DO:

1. They have joy and peace while believing (Romans 15:13, Hebrews 6:12).
2. They count God as faithful (Hebrews 11:11).
3. They speak things into existence like God (Romans 4:16-17, Mark 11:23).
4. They have confidence that God answers prayer (1 John 5:14, 15).
5. They do not fear (Isaiah 41:10; 2 Timothy 1:7).
6. They are saved (Mark 16:16).
7. They walk in forgiveness (Mark 11:25, 26).
8. They build up their faith by praying in the Holy Ghost (Jude 20).

9. They use their authority given by God (Luke 10:19).
10. They cast down ungodly thoughts (2 Corinthians 10:4, 5).
11. They are strong and courageous (Joshua 1:9).
12. They please God (Hebrews 11:6).
13. They obey God's instructions (Isaiah 1:19, 20).
14. They are patient in the middle of their problems (Romans 12:12, James 1:1-4).
15. They resist the devil (James 4:7).
16. They act on what they believe (James 2:18-20, 26).
17. They stand in the armor of God (Ephesians 6:11-18).

WHAT BELIEVERS DO NOT DO:

1. They do not get tired while doing good (Galatians 6:9).
2. They do not consider the natural to determine the reality God's promise (Romans 4:19).
3. They do not live by what they see (2 Corinthians 5:7).
4. They do not doubt (James 1:6-7, Mark 11:23).
5. They are not anxious (Philippians 4:6-8).
6. They do not complain or whine (Philippians 2:14, Romans 12:12, James 1:2).

WHAT BELIEVERS RECEIVE:

1. They receive blessings because they believe (Luke 1:45).
2. They receive the harvest of what they've been believing for (Galatians 6:9).
3. They receive the answer to their prayer (1 John 5:14, 15).
4. They receive good testimony or compliment (Hebrews 11:2).
5. They receive salvation (Romans 10:8-10).
6. They receive miracles (Hebrews 11; Mark 16:17, 18).

APPENDIX C

SCRIPTURES TO STAND ON

THE FOLLOWING ARE verses to help build your faith and keep you encouraged as you fight the good fight of faith. Faith comes by hearing and hearing by the Word of God (Romans 10:17). The more you meditate (mutter, utter, revolve in the mind) on these Scriptures, the stronger in your faith and confidence in God will become, enabling you to receive God's promises. There are many more on each of these subjects, but this will get you started on your way to victory.

WALKING IN LOVE

1 Corinthians 13 (whole chapter)

By this we know love, because He laid down His life for us. And we also ought to lay down our lives for the brethren. But whoever has this world's goods, and sees his brother in need, and shuts up his heart from him, how does the love of God abide in him? (1 John 3:16-18)

And walk in love, as Christ also has loved us and given Himself for us, an offering and a sacrifice to God for a sweet-smelling aroma (Ephesians 5:2).

Beloved, let us love one another, for love is of God; and everyone who loves is born of God and knows God. He who does not love does not know God, for God is love (1 John 4:7-8).

FORGIVENESS

"And forgive us our debts, as we forgive our debtors" (Matthew 6:12).

"And whenever you stand praying, if you have anything against anyone, forgive him, that your Father in heaven may also forgive you your trespasses" (Mark 11:25).

"Judge not, and you shall not be judged. Condemn not, and you shall not be condemned. Forgive, and you will be forgiven" (Luke 6:37).

GUIDANCE

The steps of a good man are ordered by the LORD, and He delights in his way (Psalm 37:23).

Trust in the LORD with all your heart, and lean not on your own understanding; in all your ways acknowledge Him, and He shall direct your paths (Proverbs 3:5-6).

For as many as are led by the Spirit of God, these are sons of God (Romans 8:14).

GOD KEEPS HIS WORD

Let us hold fast the confession of our hope without wavering, for He who promised is faithful (Hebrews 10:23).

"God is not a man, that He should lie, nor a son of man, that He should repent. Has He said, and will He not do? Or has He spoken, and will He not make it good?" (Numbers 23:19)

"Therefore know that the Lord your God, He is God, the faithful God who keeps covenant and mercy for a thousand generations with those who love Him and keep His commandments..." (Deuteronomy 7:9)

VICTORY

These things I have spoken to you, that in Me you may have peace. In the world you will have tribulation; but be of good cheer, I have overcome the world" (John 16:33).

Yet in all these things we are more than conquerors through Him who loved us (Romans 8:37).

But thanks be to God, who gives us the victory through our Lord Jesus Christ
(1 Corinthians 15:57).

WORRY

"Therefore I say to you, do not worry about your life, what you will eat or what you will drink; nor about your body, what you will put on. Is not life more than food and the body more than clothing?" (Matthew 6:25)

Be anxious for nothing, but in everything by prayer and supplication, with thanksgiving, let your requests be made known to God; and the peace of God, which surpasses all understanding, will guard your hearts and minds through Christ Jesus (Philippians 4:6-7).

Therefore humble yourselves under the mighty hand of God, that He may exalt you in due time, casting all your care upon Him, for He cares for you (1 Peter 5:6-7).

FEAR

Fear not, for I am with you; be not dismayed, for I am your God. I will strengthen you, yes, I will help you, I will uphold you with My righteous right hand (Isaiah 41:10).

He will not be afraid of evil tidings; his heart is steadfast, trusting in the Lord (Psalm 112:7).

For God has not given us a spirit of fear, but of power and of love and of a sound mind (2 Timothy 1:7).

PRAYER

Be anxious for nothing, but in everything by prayer and supplication, with thanksgiving, let your requests be made known to God …
(Philippians 4:6).

"For assuredly, I say to you, whoever says to this mountain, 'Be removed and be cast into the sea,' and does not doubt in his heart, but believes that those things he says will be done, he will have whatever he says. Therefore I say to you, whatever things you ask when you pray, believe that you receive them, and you will have them'"
(Mark 11:23-24).

> Now this is the confidence that we have in Him, that if we ask anything according to His will, He hears us. And if we know that He hears us, whatever we ask, we know that we have the petitions that we have asked of Him (1 John 5:14-15).

DEPRESSION

> Finally, brethren, whatever things are true, whatever things are noble, whatever things are just, whatever things are pure, whatever things are lovely, whatever things are of good report, if there is any virtue and if there is anything praiseworthy—meditate on these things (Philippians 4:8).

> Why are you cast down, O my soul? And why are you disquieted within me? Hope in God; for I shall yet praise Him, the help of my countenance and my God (Psalm 42:11).

> Therefore humble yourselves under the mighty hand of God, that He may exalt you in due time, casting all your care upon Him, for He cares for you (1 Peter 5:6-7).

GOD'S PROVISION

And my God shall supply all your need according to His riches in glory by Christ Jesus (Philippians 4:19).

"Therefore I say to you, do not worry about your life, what you will eat or what you will drink; nor about your body, what you will put on. Is not life more than food and the body more than clothing? Look at the birds of the air, for they neither sow nor reap nor gather into barns; yet your heavenly Father feeds them. Are you not of more value than they? Which of you by worrying can add one cubit to his stature? "So why do you worry about clothing? Consider the lilies of the field, how they grow: they neither toil nor spin; and yet I say to you that even Solomon in all his glory was not arrayed like one of these. Now if God so clothes the grass of the field, which today is, and tomorrow is thrown into the oven, *will He* not much more *clothe* you, O you of little faith? "Therefore do not worry, saying, 'What shall we eat?' or 'What shall we drink?' or 'What shall we wear?' For after all these things the Gentiles seek. For your heavenly Father knows that you need all these things. But seek first the kingdom of God and His righteousness, and all these things shall be added to you. Therefore do not worry about tomorrow, for tomorrow will worry about its own things. Sufficient for the day *is* its own trouble (Matthew 6:25-34).

GOD'S PROTECTION

Psalm 91 (whole chapter)

The angel of the Lord encamps all around those who fear Him, and delivers them (Psalm 34:7).

But the Lord is faithful, who will establish you and guard you from the evil one (2 Thessalonians 3:3).

And the Lord will deliver me from every evil work and preserve me for His heavenly kingdom. To Him be glory forever and ever. Amen (2 Timothy 4:18)!

TRUST

Trust in the Lord with all your heart, and lean not on your own understanding; in all your ways acknowledge Him, and He shall direct your paths (Proverbs 3:5, 6).

The Lord is my strength and my shield; my heart trusted in Him, and I am helped; therefore my heart greatly rejoices, and with my song I will praise Him (Psalm 28:7).

Some trust in chariots, and some in horses; but we will remember the name of the Lord our God (Psalm 20:7).

HEALING

Beloved, I pray that you may prosper in all things and be in health, just as your soul prospers (3 John 2).

…who Himself bore our sins in His own body on the tree, that we, having died to sins, might live for righteousness—by whose stripes you were healed (1 Peter 2:24).

He sent His word and healed them, and delivered *them* from their destructions (Psalm 107:20).

STRENGTH

Fear not, for I am with you; be not dismayed, for I am your God. I will strengthen you, yes, I will help you, I will uphold you with My righteous right hand (Isaiah 41:10).

He gives power to the weak, and to those who have no might He increases strength (Isaiah 40:29).

I will go in the strength of the Lord GOD; I will make mention of Your righteousness, of Yours only (Psalm 71:16).

APPENDIX D

REASONS NOT TO FEAR

1. He is your God and banner of victory (Isaiah 41:10, Exodus 17:15).
2. He is with you (Isaiah 41:10, Psalm 23:4).
3. God is in and upon you (2 Corinthians 6:16, Acts 1:8).
4. God is for you (Romans 8:31)
5. He has given you an inheritance of protection and deliverance (I Peter 1:3-4, Ephesians 1:11).
6. He has given you the power of the Holy Spirit (Acts 1:8).
7. He enables you with His strength (Philippians 4:13).
8. He has given His angels charge over you (Psalm 91:11).

9. He upholds, strengthens, and helps you (Isaiah 41:10).
10. He protects you from evil (Psalm 121:7-8, Psalm 91:2).
11. He is faithful and keeps His promises (Deuteronomy 7:9).
12. He has given you His Word as armor (Psalm 91:4, Ephesians 6:10-18)
13. He answers when I call (Psalm 91:15).
14. He has given you the name of Jesus (John 16:23-24, John 14:12-13).
15. He has given you authority over evil (Luke 10:19).
16. He is your father (Romans 8:15, Psalm 103:13).
17. Nothing is too hard for Him (Jeremiah 32:17, Isaiah 59:1).
18. He loves you (John 3:16)!

CONNECT WITH THE AUTHOR:

If you enjoyed this book, visit my website at christmadrid.org to get your free inspirational mini book download as well as insider updates on future book publications, blog postings, and speaking announcements.

Would you also consider rating and reviewing this book on *www.Amazon.com*? *Reviews are crucial for any author, and even just a line or two can make a huge difference.*

www.ingramcontent.com/pod-product-compliance
Lightning Source LLC
LaVergne TN
LVHW051553080426
835510LV00020B/2964